Elements of Knowledge

The Vanderbilt Library of American Philosophy offers interpretive perspectives on the historical roots of American philosophy and on present innovative developments in American thought, including studies of values, naturalism, social philosophy, cultural criticism, and applied ethics.

General Editor
Herman J. Saatkamp, Jr.
Texas A&M University

Editorial Advisory Board
Kwame Anthony Appiah *(Harvard)*
John Lachs *(Vanderbilt)*
John J. McDermott *(Texas A&M)*
Joel Porte *(Cornell)*
Hilary Putnam *(Harvard)*
Ruth Anna Putnam *(Wellesley)*
Charlene Haddock Seigfried *(Purdue)*
Beth J. Singer *(Brooklyn College)*
John J. Stuhr *(Pennsylvania State)*

OTHER RECENTLY PUBLISHED TITLES IN THE SERIES INCLUDE

Rorty and Pragmatism: The Philosopher Responds to His Critics
edited by Herman J. Saatkamp, Jr.

The Relevance of Philosophy to Life
John Lachs

The Philosophy of Loyalty
new paperback edition
Josiah Royce

The Thought and Character of William James
new paperback edition
Ralph Barton Perry

Genuine Individuals and Genuine Communities: A Roycean Public Philosophy
Jacquelyn Ann K. Kegley

The Loyal Physician: Roycean Ethics and the Practice of Medicine
Griffin Trotter

ELEMENTS OF KNOWLEDGE

Pragmatism, Logic, and Inquiry

REVISED AND EXPANDED EDITION

ARTHUR

FRANKLIN

STEWART

VANDERBILT UNIVERSITY PRESS

Nashville & London

Elements of Knowledge:
Pragmatism, Logic, and Inquiry
Lamar Philosophical Studies No. 3
© 1993 by Arthur Franklin Stewart
All rights reserved
Second Edition © 1994 by Arthur Franklin Stewart
All rights reserved

Revised and Expanded Edition
© 1997 by Vanderbilt University Press
Nashville, Tennessee 37235
All rights reserved

First printing 1997
97 98 99 00 01 02   6 5 4 3 2 1

This publication is made from recycled paper and meets the minimum requirements of American National Standard for Information Sciences—Permanence of Paper for Printed Library Materials ∞

Library of Congress Cataloging-in-Publication Data
    Stewart, Arthur Franklin.
      Elements of knowledge : pragmatism, logic, and inquiry /
    Arthur Franklin Stewart. -- Rev. and expanded ed.
          p.   cm. -- (The Vanderbilt Library of American
          philosophy)
      (Lamar philosophical studies ; no. 3)
      Includes bibliographical references and index.
      ISBN 0-8265-1303-4 (alk. paper)
      1. Knowledge, Theory of. 2. Pragmatism. 3. Reasoning.
    4. Logic.
      I. Title. II. Series. III. Series: Lamar philosophical studies ;
    no. 3.
    BD161.S684 1997
    121--dc21   97-21109
                                                          CIP

Manufactured in the United States of America

Do not block the way of inquiry.

—Charles Sanders Peirce

Contents

Preface

This book deals with the subject of pragmatism and human knowledge. Pragmatism is here seen as not only theoretically but also practically pervasive in our acquisition and development of knowledge. The book treats this universal component of knowledge in a manner accessible to any reader with an interest in human knowledge as a subject itself. One needs no special prior preparation to understand and apply the observations and analyses offered here. This is not to say, however, that either the subject of human knowledge and pragmatism or the treatment of them in the pages to follow present no challenges for the reader, for challenges there certainly are. Persistence in reading will yield understanding, and self-reflection will disclose avenues of application for that understanding. Such persistence and self-reflection will prove beneficial in proportion to the level and amount of their employment.

Thus, general readers interested in reflecting on knowledge and its relation to life at large, as well as students and academic specialists concerned more specifically with pragmatism and philosophy of knowledge, will find the contents of this work valuable. This book will also easily fit within any type of formal academic course that has, for at least part of its focus, an investigation of human knowledge itself. Such courses might well be found as offerings within the discipline of philosophy. But students enrolled in general introductory college courses or in unified core curriculum studies, as well as those less formally involved in an exploration of reasoning and the life of the mind, will also find this book useful. Thus, for example, *Elements of Knowledge* has been used for several years in Lamar University's required core course, Philosophy of Knowledge.

So, pragmatically speaking, this work should have quite wide academic applications at a variety of levels and throughout a range of formally organized disciplines and courses. More broadly still, this book's concerns with pragmatism and the philosophy of knowledge need not and should not be limited to purely classroom applications. In this spirit, what is presented here is a kind of conceptual "theme and variations" that begins with the ordinary experiences available to everyone and then, as an example of the continuum in which human knowledge develops, proceeds to illustrate what can be understood as a matter of common sense. Thus, this book will show that the experimental, trial-and-error method known as pragmatism is the common thread or common denominator in our acquisition and development of knowledge, whether in an academic, vocational, or professional setting or in life at large.

While the ideas put forward in this book, good and bad, are ultimately my responsibility, I have relied to a large extent on my understanding of philosophical pragmatism, or *pragmaticism,* as espoused by its inventor, Charles Sanders Peirce (1839–1914). In a move to counter unwarranted and undesirable modifications of his original doctrine, Peirce in 1905 coined the term *pragmaticism,* which, he claimed, "is ugly enough to be safe from kidnappers" (*CP* 5.414). We will note further details of this shift in terminology in chapter 1, where we will also examine the related subjects of the influence of William James and of nominalism. After 1905 Peirce continued to use both terms, and throughout this book we shall employ the term Peirce himself originally used, *pragmatism.* We shall also rely on his original meaning of it as an experimental method for determining the meaning of concepts.

Used here among other extracts from Peirce's enormous corpus of work are a number of citations from the manuscripts making up his Cambridge Conferences Lectures of 1898 (see Peirce 1898), which, until recently, were not available to scholars, students, or the public in a unified form. This deficiency has been elegantly rectified by Kenneth Ketner of Texas Tech University and Hilary Putnam of Harvard, with the publication of their *Reasoning and the Logic of Things* (Harvard University Press, 1992). I have noted the use of Peirce's 1898 lectures and other materials and concepts throughout the text.

Though based on a study of Peirce's philosophy of knowledge, this book is certainly not intended to be a full account of Peirce's thought. Economy and focus require the omission of certain concepts, even those that could yet prove useful to students and scholars exploring experimental "common denominators" in our knowledge. For example, his classification of the sciences, which is not examined here at all, provides an excellent organizing mechanism for knowledge systems in general.

In this new edition of *Elements of Knowledge,* I extend the application of pragmatism and human knowledge far beyond familiar academic concerns. The first chapter now includes a treatment of the debate between realism and nominalism, which extends back to the Middle Ages and yet is a matter of considerable relevance for us today. Peirce's notion of "predesignation" is likewise discussed in chapter 1 in the context of our selection of hypotheses for real testing. Also included in the first chapter is a discussion of what Peirce termed "abduction," the process by which hypotheses arise. Abduction is then placed in its proper context in what is here termed a pragmatic logic of events. In chapter 4, I have added an examination of certain concepts from the early history of computer design, in which Peirce was intimately involved. Computers are ubiquitous in the latter part of the twentieth century, and it is important for us to know something of their early development a hundred or more years ago. Finally, in chapter 6, the subjects of abduction and the pragmatic logic of events are revisited in the work of Johannes Kepler, whose writings illustrate how a pragmatic ethics of the mind truly operates. A theoretical and practical discussion of the dangers of uncriticized abduction closes the work.

Our examination of ordinary human experience, our efforts at genuine, creative learning in whatever field, and the progress and nature of academic disciplines themselves are all guided, but not dictated to, *by* pragmatism. I have provided several representative comparative readings from various disciplines to show how this is so. The substance of any unfamiliar illustrations used in such comparisons may be fleshed out by the use of dictionaries, encyclopedias, and histories of the various subjects under consideration. Other comparisons may easily be made using familiar, everyday experience and the resources of any good library. With the goal of determining where and how pragmatism may be found throughout our experience, these comparisons demonstrate that traditional boundaries of knowledge must be explored in nontraditional ways. Pragmatism, I maintain, functions as the fundamental method underlying all human knowledge, even knowledge developed through other subsidiary, adjunct, or contributing methods. I believe that this approach can aid such interdisciplinary comparisons.

Certain organizing features of this book will aid the reader in understanding its arguments and development. Each chapter begins with a headnote, a summary that provides a thumbnail sketch of the chapter to follow. A full index at the end of the book is meant to facilitate original comparisons of important concepts and their applications as they occur throughout the text. Additional uses for these features may come to mind as a natural outcome of each reader's investigations.

Itself an example of the hypothesis-confirming or hypothesis-refuting method of pragmatism, this book will only begin to fulfill its maximum value for any reader, or for any area of study in which it is employed, when *its* precepts too are actually tested as a hypothesis about human knowledge. I shall be pleased if such testing is undertaken, and especially gratified if it is successfully sustained.

Acknowledgments

My thanks go to James Muyskens, vice-chancellor for academic affairs of the State University System of Georgia, and to Professor Kenneth Laine Ketner, Peirce Professor of Philosophy at Texas Tech University, both of whom read and criticized the manuscript for this revised and expanded edition. Their criticisms were incisive and highly beneficial in the revising process. Special debts of gratitude are owed to Herman J. Saatkamp, Jr., professor of philosophy and chair of the Department of Humanities in Medicine at Texas A&M University and series editor for the Vanderbilt Library of American Philosophy, and to the director and editorial staff of Vanderbilt University Press. Their thoroughness and care in bringing this edition before readers are warmly appreciated. Special thanks go to Joseph D. Stamey, Turner Distinguished Professor of Religion and Philosophy at McMurry University, to Christopher Baker, chair of the Department of Languages, Literature, and Dramatic Arts at Armstrong State College, to Kendall Blanchard, vice-chancellor for academic affairs at the University of Tennessee at Martin, to Richard G. Marriott, chair of the Department of Psychology at Lamar University, and particularly to Charles Timothy Summerlin, vice-chancellor for academic affairs and acting provost at the University of Tennessee at Chattanooga, all of whom provided welcome comments and suggestions during the original manuscript's formative days.

The present revised and expanded edition grows out of two earlier editions. The first edition, in three printings, was published in 1993 and 1994 at the Center for Philosophical Studies of Lamar University. The second edition, in two printings, was published by Kendall/Hunt Publishing in 1994 and 1995. In the experimental spirit of pragmatism, all suggestions, questions, and criticisms regarding the revised and expanded edition will continue to be welcomed.

I am also grateful to William L. Joyce, associate university librarian for Rare Books and Special Collections at Princeton University Library for permission to duplicate the two historical diagrams used in chapter 4 (numbers 4.6 and 4.8), which are part of the Allan Marquand Papers collection of the library, and to use sections of the Marquand Papers formerly appearing in Professor Ketner's and my article, "The Early History of Computer Design: Charles Sanders Peirce and Marquand's Logical Machines," *The Princeton Library Chronicle* 45, no. 3 (1984). I am here again grateful to Joseph Stamey, who as editor of *Southwest Philosophical Studies,* gave permission to use sections of three of my articles that were published in that journal: "Peirce, Beddoes, and Pragmaticistic Abstraction: An Introduction," volume 13 (1991); "Objectivity in Peirce's Pragmaticism: Five Consequences for Relativism," volume 16 (1994); and "Peirce, Popper, and Putnam: Abduction, Reasoning, and Consequences," volume 19 (1997).

I am especially grateful to Harvard University Press and the President and Fellows of Harvard College for permission to reprint from the *Collected Papers of Charles Sanders Peirce,* edited by Charles Hartshorne, Paul Weiss, and Arthur Burks, 1931–1960; to the Institute for Studies in Pragmaticism of Texas Tech University for copies of Peirce's manuscripts used here; and to the Philosophy Department of Harvard University for permission to cite from the Peirce manuscripts at Houghton Library. For their cooperation in these regards, special thanks go to Beth Kiley Kinder and Judith Michelman at Harvard University Press; Kenneth Ketner of Texas Tech University; and Hilary Putnam, the Walter Beverly Pearson Professor of Modern Mathematics and Mathematical Logic at Harvard University.

Abbreviations and Editorial Practices

A version of the scientific style of reference, otherwise known as the author/date system, is used in this book. Parenthetical references include the author's name, the date of the publication in question, and numbers for the pages involved. Using the name and date, the reader will find the full bibliographic citation to any work in question in the references section at the end of the book. Four general exceptions to this author/date scheme are keyed to the following abbreviations:

CP   C. S. Peirce, *Collected Papers of Charles Sanders Peirce*, 8 vols. in 4, ed. Charles Hartshorne, Paul Weiss, and Arthur Burks (Cambridge: Harvard University Press, 1931 . . . 1960). References are cited by volume and paragraph numbers.

MS   Peirce manuscripts in the Houghton Library at Harvard University. These citations are referenced according to the dates and manuscript numbers given in Robin 1967, *Annotated Catalogue of the Papers of Charles S. Peirce*, and the pagination established by the Institute for Studies in Pragmaticism of Texas Tech University.

NEM   C. S. Peirce, *The New Elements of Mathematics*, 4 vols. in 5, ed. Carolyn Eisele (The Hague: Mouton, 1976). References are cited by volume and page numbers.

RLT   C. S. Peirce, *Reasoning and the Logic of Things: The Cambridge Conferences Lectures of 1898*, ed. Kenneth Laine Ketner and Hilary Putnam (Cambridge: Harvard University Press, 1992). References are cited by page numbers. Manuscripts for *RLT* are located in the Bibliography under Peirce 1898.

Although the reader may find the spelling, punctuation, and style of some of the extracts quoted from Peirce to be quaint or odd, these

usages are preserved here in their original forms to maintain historical accuracy. Except where otherwise indicated, all materials in brackets are my own.

1

What Is Pragmatism, and What Is Its Value?

■ *Pragmatism is a fundamental method for knowing and determining the meaning of those persistent realities that we, following Peirce, term facts (CP 1.175) and, subsequently, the veracity of our statements about these facts. Pragmatism is equivalent to the basic experimental procedures of the laboratory sciences, but it may be employed in any field of knowledge or area of life. Its three-part structure is defined as identifying the problem; offering an explanatory hypothesis through abductive means; and testing our hypothesis against the problem by deductive means, especially so as to eliminate with certainty our hypothesis should it prove erroneous. Any surviving hypothesis will, by inductive means, give probable and perhaps reliable results. Closely associated with the American philosopher Charles Sanders Peirce, pragmatism relies on the doctrine of realism, that is, critical observations of real objects of knowledge independent of personal opinion, in contrast to nominalism, a doctrine that is more subjective in determining the nature of things. Pragmatism encourages a disciplined ethics of the mind that engages in the critical testing and elimination of error in matters ranging, for example, from the basic mechanics of walking, to the principles of geometry, to the evolving theories and practical applications of medical science. As this chapter will show, it is a process that never ceases.*

P RAGMATISM IS A method, synonymous with the experimental method of the sciences, for acquiring and developing human knowledge. So claimed the inventor of pragmatism as a philosophical doctrine, the American philosopher, mathematician, scientist, and logician Charles

Sanders Peirce (1839–1914). The mere mention of science will probably make some readers of this book a little nervous, just as any implied
expectations about mathematics will, for many, provoke outright fear.
But why this nervousness and fear? Consider these two descriptive
propositions from the fields of science and mathematics: Water boils at
212 degrees on the Fahrenheit scale, and 2 + 2 = 4. Few people would
express nervousness or fear over these basic concepts from science and
mathematics, largely because they already know how to perform the
experiments that verify the accuracy of these two statements.

But suppose that our statements under question were more complex or abstract. Suppose they asserted a sociological notion embodied
in ancient Egyptian art that led those artists to vary from literal realism, or a theological notion embedded in Medieval cathedral art that
led those artists to discard realism altogether. In those cases, you very
well might not have the experiments ready and at hand to show yourself the complete accuracy of the assertions. Yet the basic experimental procedure of pragmatism is *exactly* the same in all four of these examples from science, mathematics, and art history: you must first
create an explanation that will survive testing.

The basic model of this procedure may be described as follows: (1)
identify the problem at hand; (2) create a predictive explanation or explanatory hypothesis to explain the problem; (3) test your explanation
or hypothesis against the problem for conclusive results. We may summarize this three-part procedure as Problem-Hypothesis-Test (PHT).
This experimental model of pragmatism operates throughout the experience of human knowledge.

Of course, much of our experience of human knowledge is not, in
the specialized and quasi-formal sense of the organized laboratory sciences, "scientific." Rather it includes ordinary matters of life at large.
Whether these matters fit within particular academic disciplines or
other organized areas of knowledge, the PHT process addresses how
we truly learn about anything at all.

Elimination of an erroneous hypothesis means that the hypothesis
or predictive explanation in question is found inconsistent with or
contradictory to features of the problem it was alleged to explain. This

erroneous hypothesis, then, is dropped or eliminated from our consideration. As diagram 1.1 implies, this testing of what we say we know, overall, against that which is yet to be known, and this testing of our beliefs, overall, against the objective truths that we know about them *never ceases*.

This PHT method of pragmatism, then, can be diagrammed for ease of inspection as follows: "P" is the problem at hand, "H" is a hypothesis that may or may not help explain it, "T" is a test of a hypothesis, "x" indicates the elimination, through testing, of an erroneous hypothesis or explanation or belief, and "?" indicates a surviving hypothesis, explanation, or belief that, while having survived our testing and thus bearing a certain degree of trustworthiness, may *yet still* be eliminated.

With a problem identified, then, and with hypotheses germane to it in hand, the logic of our comparison of hypotheses against problems can be visualized and diagrammed as follows, where, again, "x" indicates the elimination with certainty of erroneous hypotheses and "?" indicates provisional approval. Following from left to right in this diagram, we see that explanatory hypotheses tested against the problem or problems they are alleged to explain will either survive probabilistically into the future or be discarded with certainty as a result of the test. As an illustration, we can use the problem of determining the ordinary boiling point of water and four different hypotheses as possible solutions to this problem.

Diagram 1.1

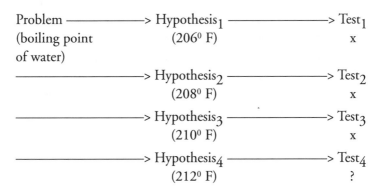

$$Problem \longrightarrow Hypothesis_1 \longrightarrow Test_1$$
$$(boiling\ point \qquad (206^0\ F) \qquad x$$
$$of\ water)$$

$$\longrightarrow Hypothesis_2 \longrightarrow Test_2$$
$$(208^0\ F) \qquad x$$

$$\longrightarrow Hypothesis_3 \longrightarrow Test_3$$
$$(210^0\ F) \qquad x$$

$$\longrightarrow Hypothesis_4 \longrightarrow Test_4$$
$$(212^0\ F) \qquad ?$$

It should be noted that while we reach a kind of practical certainty with our fourth hypothesis above, *logically* our testing of it, as with other successful hypotheses, recommences whenever we again employ it.

The basic structure of biological evolution through natural selection is a living example of the pragmatic process. Let us posit a workable understanding of natural selection as follows: Some genetic stocks, over time, in competition with their environment, are more or less successful than others at survival and reproductive transmission of their genetically based characteristics. Using evolution by natural selection as an example of pragmatism, our basic Problem—Hypothesis—Test structure can be filled out as follows:

P = The general *problem* is whether or not a given genetic stock, the human species, let us say, will survive against the environment in which it functions;

H = Our *hypothesis* is that this particular genetic stock, the human species, will so survive;

T = Let us *test* H against P and observe the results, paying closest attention to the individuals or groups, according to diagram 1.1, above, that get eliminated, that turn out to be, in a general sense, errors.

Thus, with biological evolution as our present illustration, we can see that the method of pragmatism extends far beyond the confines of human knowledge itself and, in a fundamental biological sense, is a 'reality', a 'real' object beyond our personal opinions or actual control.

The doctrine that there are such real objects of knowledge and that such reality is independent of our purely personal opinions or egotistic whims is called realism. Realism claims that trees or rocks and other existing things are real, but that in addition there are also abstract or non-concrete objects, like gravity or beauty, that are also real even though, for example, you cannot touch them. This view makes sense, upon reflection. We all acknowledge that the realities we term *gravity* and *beauty* function independently of our whims, however much we may disagree about exactly what these terms mean. These objects of knowledge *are there*, in the cosmos, in nature. But they do not exist in the sense of your being able to give to someone else a handful of gravity or of beauty.

In contrast, the doctrine of nominalism, that there are no real objects independent of human thought, including our personal opinions or egotistical wishes—in either of the senses described above—says that we ascribe names to things like gravity, not to point out realities but to give titles to collections of properties that we have assembled for our purposes. So, roughly put, the realist, on the one hand, would say that we acknowledge things like trees and rocks, or gravity and beauty because they are real objects that are independent of our wishes, that are persistent in reality or nature, and that influence us considerably yet are not themselves influenced by our desires as to what the nature of their properties or characteristics are or should be. Things with such real persistence Peirce termed *facts* (*CP* 1.173; 1.175). The nominalist, on the other hand, would say that such examples are but instances of collected properties or characteristics of what we consider to be trees and rocks, or gravity and beauty, to which we have assigned special names but which are, in fact, nothing more than names for collections of our private experiences.

You can see that while *realism* seems at first to be confusing and fantastical, *nominalism* invites us to *make up our reality just as we please*, assigning names to collections of properties according to whatever suits our private purposes. Thus, nominalism turns out to be a rather dangerous doctrine for the acquisition and development of human knowledge. For if I assign the name *honesty* to properties X, and Y, and Z, while you assign the name *honesty* to properties not-X, and not-Y, and not-Z, we will find ourselves unable to decide which of us has the more accurate understanding of *honesty*, except by means such as which of us can summon the greater amount of persuasive force, of whatever kind.

Realism, which was a basic tenet of C. S. Peirce, the inventor of pragmatism as a philosophical doctrine, is fundamental to our understanding here. In his sense of things, realities are not independent of our thought *altogether*, for if they were, how could we come to know them? But realities *are* independent of our arbitrary or egotistic thought, which is to say that *we do not make up the objects of our knowledge*, however mundane or sophisticated they may be. Let us look into how our PHT construct relies on realism.

Any substantive test forces examination of our explanation or hypothesis against the *problem involved*, thus highlighting a certain aspect of our understanding of reality, for results. Every substantive problem that we notice and attempt to solve by test thus actually represents a window on reality and asks two questions, namely:

(1) Is the theory or set of fundamental beliefs with which we are proceeding in this moment of testing still intact after we have concluded our test? Has the problem and our attempted solutions to it left our fundamental beliefs or base sense of reality unchanged, or does it invite change in our assumptions about reality?

(2) Does this proposed, hypothetical solution explain our immediate problem or not?

When the subject of our inquiries is the nature of reality itself, we are dealing with the branch of knowledge known as metaphysics. When the subject is human knowledge itself, we are dealing with epistemology, or the philosophy of knowledge. What we are doing in this book is taking human knowledge *itself* as a subject of study. Clearly, if our fundamental assumptions about reality, our metaphysics, are of a nominalistic character, our knowledge will follow suit in the objectionable fashion shown in our illustration of the nominalistic meanings of *honesty*. But let us return to the two questions asked above.

There are any number of examples from the histories of various pursuits that illustrate how question (1) can result in fundamental changes in one's metaphysics, and how answering question (2) can lead to such fundamental changes. The development during the nineteenth century of the modern understanding of infectious disease, which rendered absurd the old and venerated humoral theory of disease, is one such example of both sorts of answers. The humoral theory, with its technique of bloodletting as a supposed curative measure, simply did not rid people of disease processes. With any patient or immediate problem of disease confronting the humoral physician, question (2) was answered in the negative. This led, eventually and in the following way, to a change in belief about reality and our place in it.

The fundamental set of beliefs or base sense of reality that had sustained the humoral theory as accepted medical wisdom for over two thousand years was an inaccurate one. It said in effect that disease was a process that arose *within* us from supposed "imbalances" in various bodily fluids. To correct such imbalances, it was believed that various amounts of these fluids needed to be removed, thus restoring overall balance and the state of health it allegedly produced. As we now know, of course, this theory *never solved the problem* that each patient represented. With the arrival of the germ theory of disease and our developing knowledge of microorganisms, together with their possible means of transmission and their likely actions on our own bodies, we equipped ourselves with a theory that *can and does solve the problem* of illnesses of microbial derivation. With this theory, we employ a set of fundamental beliefs different from what the humoral theory could allow. With the germ theory, our base sense of reality must account for *infection*, that is, for the agents of some disease processes arising *outside* of us, invading our physiologies, and causing illness. This puts us in a different status vis-à-vis disease, and it requires of us a modified base sense of reality acknowledging that we are often the objects or targets *of* infection. In the face of this modification, it would be absurd to return to the older theory, where disease arose solely from within us because of humoral imbalance.

It is important to note here that every exercise of pragmatic experimentation, however mundane or sophisticated, implies that we have for ourselves a certain base sense of reality, a certain theory about what the world is composed of and how it behaves, a certain set of fundamental beliefs about *what* we think we know and about *how* we know what we think we know. In addition to our conscious modifications of our knowledge, many of our basic beliefs are unconsciously inherited. All of us have such sets of acquired and inherited fundamental beliefs, regardless of who or where we are, sometimes quite similar to those of others, sometimes not. We hold such basic beliefs even to the point of being unconscious of them most of the time.

Disturbances in our experience and understanding of reality, those moments when our fundamental beliefs do not match the reality addressed by our beliefs, those spasms of doubt about what we think we know—these we call problems. Thus, acknowledging such disturbances and the fundamental doubts they engender, we must conclude that *our knowledge is fallible; our knowledge is capable of error*. Defining disease in terms of humoral theory is an example of such a disturbance, a moment, a spasm. It is difficult for us to understand why humoralists persisted in their erroneous belief for more than two millennia. After all, their comparison of "knowledge with reality," to abbreviate the matter, never resulted in anything other than an utter failure of what they considered knowledge. Why, in the face of repeated, incessant failure did they persist with such an absurd theory? Surely they considered their knowledge *infallible!* Even mathematics, according to Peirce, has a fallibilistic character as we employ it:

In practice, and in fact, mathematics is not exempt from that liability to error that affects everything that man does. Strictly speaking, it is not [humanly] certain that twice two is four. If on an average in every thousand figures obtained by addition by the average man there be one error, and if a thousand million men have each added 2 to 2 ten thousand times, there is still a possibility that they have all committed the same error of addition every time. . . . The certainty of mathematical reasoning, however, lies in this, that once an error is suspected, the whole world [of investigators] is speedily in accord with it. (*CP* 5.577)

Peirce's remarks point up a distinction we should bear in mind in our work here, a distinction between *practical* certainty, as when we routinely take the sum of 2 and 2 to be 4, and *ideal* certainty, as when we notice and correct mistakes in performing addition according to ideal background principles. His point is that we as human beings, as investigators of various problems, are *fallible*. In this work we shall sustain our investigations and improvements in our knowledge according to practical results, assuredly, but also with ideal background principles guiding us to note and correct errors in our methods.

Now, in addition to our *assuming* that reality works in a certain way, including our unconscious assumptions, every substantive experiment *tests* our understanding of reality. Repeated failures or inadequacies in hypothetical explanations like the humoral theory of disease urge us to look more deeply into our assumptions about reality and adjust those assumptions to better match our experiences *of* that reality. The history of the humoral theory discloses that to become thoroughly and egotistically wedded to a particular theory invites warped, inaccurate views of reality and inadequate, defective knowledge that results from such views. This history also discloses that the biggest and most formidable obstacles to improving human knowledge are not things like present ignorance or the present lack of investigative technique, both of which are unavoidable at times anyway, but rather a poor system of mental ethics, by which the uncontrolled ego will choose hypotheses unwisely or not actually *choose* any new ones at all, and will value the maintaining of pet theories *more than improving knowledge!* The ethics of the mind we are now seeking to develop, a *pragmatic* ethics of the mind, enjoins us to engage in *criticism*: to eliminate, by test, our errors.

We shall have occasion below to consider again and in greater detail the humoral theory of disease, but before we pause in our considerations of it, an additional observation will be valuable: the uncontrolled ego invites us to make up our reality just as we please.

In our pragmatic testing, then, we must acknowledge a fundamental reality as our persisting environment, however vague or even inaccurate our understanding of that reality may be for the present. We seek, by test, to understand that reality better. And when our beliefs are inconsistent with or even contradictory to that reality, we must modify our beliefs, that is, we improve our knowledge. If belief conflicts with reality, it is belief that must go.

We can, with proper information, clear-headed reasoning, and a creative approach, improve or change our knowledge. But reality we do not change, nor do we "make it up," as it were. Here is how Peirce described reality, or 'the real', in his "Some Consequences of Four Incapacities."

The real, then, is that which, sooner or later, information and reasoning would finally result in, and which is therefore *independent of the vagaries of me and you*. Thus, the very origin or the conception of reality shows that this conception essentially involves the notion of a COMMUNITY, without definite limits, and capable of a definite increase of knowledge. (CP 5.311; emphasis added).

Note especially that he does not say that the real is entirely independent of our thought but that it is independent of the "vagaries" or egotistic whims of us. It is crucial to our understandings here that we acknowledge reality to have a life of its own: it goes right ahead with its activities regardless of our opinions, tastes, or what we think we know about it. In his 1877 "The Fixation of Belief"—the first of six papers gathered under the title "Illustrations of the Logic of Science," for the *Popular Science Monthly*—Peirce gave the following summary of these ideas about reality, its autonomy, the method of pragmatism, and the communitarian or public nature of truth and knowledge about reality. (In this extended extract, two additional remarks by Peirce from 1903 are included in brackets.)

To satisfy our doubts, therefore, it is necessary that a method should be found by which our beliefs may be determined by nothing human, but by some external permanency—by something upon which our thinking has no effect. [But which, on the other hand, unceasingly tends to influence thought;

or, in other words, by something real.] Some mystics imagine that they have such a method in a private inspiration from on high. But that is only a form of the method of tenacity, in which the conception of truth as something public is not yet developed. Our external permanency would not be external, in our sense, if it was restricted in its influence to one individual. It must be something which affects, or might affect, every man. And, though these affections are necessarily as various as are individual conditions, yet the method must be such that the ultimate conclusion of every man shall be the same. [Or would be the same if inquiry were sufficiently persisted in.] Such is the method of science. Its fundamental hypothesis, restated in more familiar language, is this: There are real things, whose characters are entirely independent of our opinions about them; those realities affect our senses according to regular laws, and, though our sensations are as different as our relations to the objects, yet, by taking advantage of the laws of perception, we can ascertain by reasoning how things really are; and any man, if he have sufficient experience and reason enough about it, will be led to the one True conclusion. The new conception here involved is that of reality. (*CP* 5.384)

What sorts of things qualify as such realities? What sorts of things maintain an external permanency, influence thought but are independent of egotistic thought, and are the sorts of knowledge-items that continued investigation should bring us all into agreement about? That there is such a real as gravity, however quantified and described, would seem to qualify. Likewise, the heliocentric model of the solar system certainly fits Peirce's prescription for a real object. A stone fits too, as does the valid syllogistic forms of argument we shall consider later. That every number has a double and that this double is divisible by two, Boyle's Law linking the pressure of a gas and its volume, the Law of non-Contradiction, and that pianos have eighty-eight keys all seem to be realities. Continued investigation would bring scientifically minded persons—which is to say, fundamentally, persons whose egos are controlled—into agreement about these things. These objects influence what we think we know. But what we think we know *does not* influence them, and they certainly have a kind of external permanency about them.

Yet, can we consider beauty too to be such a real object? Should or could honesty be added to the list? And what about morality? In such cases as these last three, it may perhaps be advisable to consider our progress toward increasing the knowledge of realities, especially the truly elusive ones like beauty, honesty, and morality, rather in the manner that the pianist Artur Schnabel (1882–1951) saw the experimentalism required of musical artistry. He thought that in music we continue our experiments "from seemingly simple and modest aspirations by way of increasing (even frightening) complications . . . toward that other shore which, to be sure, can only be sighted but never reached" (Schnabel 1942: 14). Schnabel's shore was the reality of artistic perfection, an elusive reality but one nevertheless eminently worthy of unflagging pursuit.

We come to know reality better by pragmatic or evolutionary means, and we defend against becoming self-centered in our beliefs and knowledge about reality by comparing our beliefs, conclusions, and methods with those of others in our investigative community. We shall shortly take up the characteristics of those equipped to belong to such a community of investigators, a community of scientifically minded persons. The important thing here is to recognize that our knowledge of reality, our own self-criticisms, and the criticisms of our fellow investigators combine to form an environment for our knowledge that will eliminate over time those explanatory hypotheses that turn out to be inconsistent or contradictory with reality, with the real. *Criticism* here means the pragmatic elimination of error. Our acknowledgment of realism makes pragmatic, evolutionary criticism possible and sustainable. We keep testing our knowledge against the standard of the real, knowing that without this elusive standard our criticisms become mere personal, subjective squabblings. Just as a poorly adapted species will, evolutionarily, be eliminated by its environment, so erroneous hypotheses, pragmatically, will be eliminated from our stock of beliefs and knowledge.

It is this evolutionary or Darwinian character of pragmatic acquisition and development of human knowledge that led Sir Karl
Popper (1902–1994), the eminent philosopher of science, to make
the following interdisciplinary remarks in "The Rationality of
Scientific Revolutions," his Herbert Spencer Lecture of 1973:

> Of course, I do conjecture that Darwinism is right, even on the level of sci-
> entific discovery; and that it is right even beyond this level: that *it is right even
> on the level of artistic creation*. We do not discover new facts or new effects by
> copying them. . . . We use, rather, the method of trial and the elimination
> of error. As Ernst Gombrich says, "making comes before matching": the ac-
> tive production of a new trial structure comes before its exposure to elimi-
> nating tests. (Miller 1985: 85–86; my italics)

The phrase "We do not discover new facts or new effects by copying them" is extraordinarily important. To say that we discover or
learn anything by merely copying what has been put in front of us or
what has been set up as an unmodifiable doctrine amounts to two
things that we should avoid: (1) a rote, mechanicalistic, or "trained
parrot" approach to so-called learning, and (2) a dogmatic, unadapt-
able, or purely doctrinal approach to so-called knowledge. The former
we are all familiar with in the syndrome of memorizing items of information just long enough to complete an examination of some sort.
The latter we have all encountered in our sometimes stubborn denials
in the face of clear evidence, let us say about an emotional relationship, that makes our belief in the matter, *right then*, to be an error. A
rote, dogmatic approach to knowledge is doomed in two respects: (1)
it cannot create new trials to test alleged instances of human knowledge, and (2) it cannot eliminate errors, that is, it cannot *correct itself*
as pragmatism does. Clearly, for legitimate knowledge, we *MUST* perform the evolutionary act of knowing in our own minds and in our
own imaginations.

The following three examples of a pragmatic, experimental, self-
correcting approach to knowledge deal with, respectively, ordinary life

at large (walking), how we learn a new subject (geometry), and the processes and natures of academic disciplines or other organized departments of study themselves (in this case, medicine).

Consider, for a moment, how we came to know how to walk as a commonplace example of pragmatism in action. Who can recall how many trials we proposed for ourselves to overcome the obvious problem, and who can recount how many erroneous physiological hypotheses were eliminated during the testing process? Did we not self-correct these errors? And do we not, still, every time we walk across the room, continue the experiment? Does this experiment, during our lifetime, or the lifetime of human beings as a species, *ever cease?* Already at this point, perhaps, you can fill out our PHT model of pragmatism with walking as an illustration.

Our second example, dealing with the pragmatic approach we use whenever we learn anything new, deals with Euclidean geometry. Specifically, this illustration deals with the fourth proposition of the first book of Euclid's *Elements of Geometry.* This proposition states that if a pair of sides and the interior angle produced by these sides in a scalene triangle are equal to the respective sides and angle of another triangle, (1) the remaining side and the two additional angles of one will be equal to the respective side and angles of the other, and (2) the two completed respective triangles themselves will also be equal to each other. All this depends on the primitive truth or "beginning assumption" or, to use the technical term, the *axiom* that things which coincide with one another are equal to one another.

How would our PHT model be filled out using what we wish to learn here about Euclid as our illustration? The overall problem, generally, can be expressed in the question, How can I understand and thereby learn this? The "this" is in at least five parts: (1) understanding the comparison given in the axiom, (2) understanding the similarity of the two given scalene triangles, (3) understanding the relation between the remaining third sides, (4) understanding the relation between the remaining third pairs of angles, and (5) understanding the congruence between the two completed triangles. Our overall problem, then, is in five parts or subproblems, each inviting attempted hypothetical solutions.

The overall hypothesis that we can make for ourselves actually implies two large and competing hypotheses, each of which contains any number of testable hypotheses or predictive explanations: (1) If I merely "copy" into my memory the right phrases and technical terms, and repeat them mindlessly until the examination is completed, then I will truly have understood this! or (2) I believe I need to make some experimental comparisons, probably by trial and error, of what geometrical, dimensional equivalence actually *is* as a real relation; for that relation seems to be the general problem adressed by this particular geometrical problem. If I can get a grasp on that in each of these five parts, and in the overall process or demonstration as a whole, then I might actually see why, given the first four items in order, the congruence of the two scalene triangles produced *is inevitable!* This second hypothesis involves our five subhypotheses, which, if successful, will bring us to a genuine understanding of Euclid's proposition. Euclid guides us towards choosing or guessing at the best hypothesis with his remarks, but in the end it is our own creative act of association of the triangles' parts that brings us to successful subhypotheses, their successful tests, and our successful understanding of the two triangles' overall congruence.

As with learning how to walk, who can say how many trials and errors will be self-corrected in the process of testing solutions to problems in geometry? Each one of our experimental comparisons here, as in learning how to walk, will be a hypothesis, an explanation, a prediction that we speak to ourselves saying, "*This* approach might work." Any individual speculation, therefore, may or may not survive being tested against the problem. Once we have found a series of such explanations that successfully brings us to the conclusion of Euclid's demonstration, we then have a general tactic for further study of Euclidean geometry. And every time we use that tactic, whether in Euclidean geometry or in another area where a mathematical approach might be useful, we will be, yet again, *continuing the experiment.*

Our third example of pragmatism in action deals with medicine or, better, a speciality within medicine known as pathology, the study of disease. Here we shall see how an academic discipline or organized department of study is *itself* guided by, and proceeds in its increase in knowledge by, pragmatic means. Here, for our PHT schema, the problem, obviously, is disease itself. We will look at three different historical hypotheses for treating disease, only one of which, upon serious testing, turned out to be of any value.

The first of these is the so-called humoral theory of disease mentioned above, to which we will now devote more detailed investigation. This theory came down from the Greeks of the fifth century B.C. and was elevated to the status of dogma in the second century A.D. by the Roman physician Galen, who claimed that all disease was due to an imbalance between four basic fluids or bodily "humors." These four humors were also associated with certain parts of the body. Thus, the humor phlegm was paired with the brain, yellow bile with the liver, black bile with the spleen, and, most importantly for our purposes, blood was paired with itself.

We modern-minded people would think it strange if someone said that disease was caused, in some cases, by a comparative surplus of blood, but this was exactly what the humoral theory claimed for large numbers of patients. Thus, from antiquity until the late eighteenth century, a standard procedure for the treatment of diseases of many kinds was to bleed the patient. Make no mistake, this was serious business: Boccaccio's *Decameron* includes a depiction of a fellow undergoing this treatment by having fourteen leeches attached to his upper torso and arms! Remarkably, it seems that some people knew that this procedure and others like it were not actually "working." For example, in his letter seeking a second opinion from someone other than the local physicians then treating him, Peter the Venerable, Abbot of Cluny in the mid-twelfth century, makes plain that he did not find reasonable the sorts of curative tactics he was enduring (see Duin and Sutcliffe 1992). Could the humoral theory of disease have survived in a pragmatic testing sequence like the one outlined in diagram 1.1 (p. 3), where erroneous explanations, by their persistent failures, are eliminated?

The second hypothesis concerning disease was the so-called "miasmatic" theory. It was the most popular theory of disease at the midpoint of the nineteenth century, holding that disease was caused by the fumes given off by decaying matter. Can you imagine, as a thought experiment, what sort of testing sequence might reveal how reasonable or unreasonable this miasmatic theory was as an explanatory hypothesis of disease? Well, the French Academy of Sciences did, in the following rather roundabout way.

An item of "knowledge" that captured a great deal of attention during the nineteenth century was the notion of so-called "spontaneous generation." By this process, it was claimed, lower forms of life were generated spontaneously from decaying matter. For example, because one could often find a conjunction between decaying organic matter and the appearance of flies, a cause-and-effect relation was assumed, which insisted that decaying matter spontaneously gave rise to flies. To put the matter bluntly, it was thought that rotting flesh generated or created flies.

The French Academy proposed a competition between proponents and opponents of the theory of spontaneous generation to settle this matter. Louis Pasteur (1822–1895), who had already demonstrated the role of microorganisms in the fermentation of wine and beer, now proposed the role of germs in organic decay. From there it was a small step to suppose that perhaps *disease* too was caused by such microorganisms. Going one step further, Joseph Lister (1827–1912) took this possibility seriously enough to introduce carbolic acid as an antiseptic solution. As the historian of science Jack Meadows put it, "The skirmishes over spontaneous generation led to the science of bacteriology and the germ theory of disease" (Meadows 1989: 177). Here then, at long last, was an explanatory hypothesis about the cause of disease that not only could actually *be* tested but that also *survived* being tested.

These three theories, whether erroneous or not, all had a role to play in the advance of pathology *as a discipline itself*. We can look back on all of this business about humoral, miasmatic, and germ theories of disease and easily draw the fallacious conclusion that knowledge grows in a straight, easily predictable line. But was there actually a straight, steady line of progress linking Galen with his predecessors and with Pasteur? Is a clean, straight line of progress being followed in the more contemporary pathology of HIV?

That knowledge, in any area, does not advance in a neat, predictable pattern should be clear; the humoral theory itself discloses this. With the humoral theory, it is likely that no real testing took place for better than two thousand years. Yet the attempt was persistently being made, however clumsily, to solve the problem of disease.

Although some testing *was* conducted on application of the humoral theory, none was given to the *real problem,* namely *the theory or hypothesis itself.* Practitioners of bleeding apparently never questioned the theory itself, only the technological aspects of applying the theory. Thus, one can easily imagine some dogmatic advocate of the humoral theory, having just bled some poor soul to death, beginning an explanatory mental experiment by supposing something like, "Well, it *would* have worked if we'd just used different leeches or a bigger razor or if we'd just gotten to the patient a little earlier!" and so forth. Clearly, they were not identifying the *right problem.* There is a difference, after all, between the experimental *method* of science or pragmatism and the technologies (whether leeches or lasers) we sometimes use in attempts to apply this method. Because the humoral theory persisted for so long, we have to conclude that its advocates' understanding of applied technologies and underlying scientific or pragmatic methods were badly mixed up.

Eventually, the fallacies of the humoral theory were self-corrected by the discipline itself. With this example from pathology as an illustation, we may ask a fundamental question, When reality conflicts with our explanations of it, shall we sustain our explanations or accept reality? In this case, the successful hypothetical solution was borrowed or transposed from an apparently completely different department of knowledge. This underscores what Peirce said about disciplines, that at their best they function as what he termed a "community of investigators." Such a community may and often does borrow explanations from other areas and other communities. A community of investigators consists of individuals who (1) have a genuine "Will to Learn," as Peirce put it in his fourth Cambridge Conferences Lecture (Peirce 1898, MS 442: 15; *RLT*: 170–171), (2) basically understand how to set up a legitimate testing procedure and the questions that such a procedure discloses, and, most importantly, (3) have their egoistic desires in any such pragmatic procedure well under control. The length of time involved in the passage from the humoral to the miasmatic to the modern germ theory of disease makes plain that generations of *communities* of investigators may be required to understand great problems fully. This should again remind us that pragmatic testing must *never cease*. How else can we assure ourselves today, for instance in the case of HIV, that *we* are not, with this particular knowledge problem, beginning a two-thousand-year-long folly?

What of the miasmatic theory? In considering its tenets, it is indeed hard to imagine how real testing could have taken place, even if the experimental will had been present to conduct such work. Again, the attempt was at least being made to solve a problem. But even as the humoral theory was a "dud," so was the miasmatic theory. Yet both duds contributed, in different ways, to the eventual rise of the germ theory of disease. Looking at pathology as a discipline, we can maintain that both the humoral and the miasmatic explanations were *mistakes to be made and eliminated* and, indeed, were mistakes that *HAD* to be made *before* they could be eliminated.

These examples from various aspects of ordinary life (the process of walking, learning something about Euclidean geometry, and the progress of the discipline of pathology) should help us understand how pragmatism works and should make plain something of its universal scope. A bit of history about pragmatism itself will also be useful.

Pragmatism, philosophically speaking, was invented a little over a century ago by C. S. Peirce, who many still consider to be America's greatest native intellect. In 1905 Peirce coined a new, expanded word for his approach: pragmati*cism*. Is pragmaticism somehow different from pragmatism itself? It may be useful here to provide a short account concerning the evolution of the concept of pragmatism and Peirce's re-coinage of the term as *pragmaticism* at the beginning of the twentieth century.

⋏   William James (1842–1910), sometimes referred to as the father of American psychology and often cited as Peirce's great benefactor, modified Peirce's original doctrine of pragmatism. Whereas Peirce had originally defined pragmatism as an experimental theory of the *meaning* of intellectual concepts, James defined pragmatism as a theory of *truth* in human actions.

Meaning and *truth* are seemingly two very different things. For example, we would all like to have in hand a reasonably stable meaning of 'honesty' before deciding whether or not the proposition "person X is dishonest" is true. And you certainly would not want to base your own meaning of honesty exclusively on the individual cases of honesty or dishonesty with which you are directly familiar. To derive meaning in this manner would invite nominalism and its inwardly inconsistent and dangerous nature into the search for knowledge. As we noted above, if we use only the individual cases of honesty with which we are familiar to compose a meaning for 'honesty', we invite unpleasant consequences. Again, if we assign the name *honesty* to chosen properties X, and Y, and Z, while another group assigns the name *honesty* to chosen properties not-X, and not-Y, and not-Z, we will find ourselves at loggerheads over the meaning of 'honesty'. The only apparent way consistent with nominalism to resolve this disagreement is by some use of force. And this, obviously, will not count as experimentally discovered *knowledge*, but rather as *enforced opinion!*

So Peirce, thirty-odd years after announcing pragmatism as a distinct doctrine, decided to change the name of his experimental method to the intentionally odd term *pragmaticism*. He continued afterwards to use both terms, *pragmatism* and *pragmaticism*. To avoid possible confusion, we shall generally confine our own usage here to *pragmatism*, remembering that it is Peirce's meaning that we are after, regardless of the term. No matter which term is used, what we seek is the best possible method we can muster for the detection and elimination of error in our beliefs, our habits, and our knowledge, however those beliefs, habits, and "knowledge" came to us in what we take to be the first place.

Karl Popper was delighted to acknowledge several years ago that he and Peirce arrived at some startlingly similar views. Popper puts this whole matter of "What Is Pragmatism, and What Is Its Value?" in a nutshell, one with two parts, to which we will add a third. First, Popper credits the ancient Greek Xenophanes to have thought, felt, believed, and actually *known* something rather profound about knowledge itself: "Xenophanes knew that our knowledge is guesswork" (Miller 1985: 52). That is, when we come up with explanations for our problems, however ordinary or high-flown they may appear, we might, after all, just be guessing! To this we should say: "So what?" After all, given that we cannot know the future until it becomes the present, is not *any* prediction about the future, *any* explanatory hypothesis, strictly speaking, a guess? Second, Popper offers a pragmatic challenge in his remark: "*How can we hope to detect and eliminate error?*" (Miller 1985: 52; Popper's italics.) That is, whatever the consequences of our wildest guesses, irrational hopes, most cold-blooded logical conclusions, warm-hearted sympathies, ignorances, arrogances, and all the rest of what we might call our explanations and assumptions, we must *compare these consequences against what we think those consequences will explain to us.* This then is an issue of mental ethics, of being willing to test the consequences of our beliefs or explanations, particularly when doubt arises, of testing them against their real backgrounds. Third, using human judgment rather than merely mechanical calculations, test your explanations *and* assumptions against those problems that your explanations and assumptions are supposed to solve! And, of course, continue such testing unceasingly.

So, to summarize our investigations in a general but formal way, the basic structure of the method of pragmatism for the acquisition and development of human knowledge amounts to the following three items. But always keep in mind that pragmatism is a *method*. And methods are clearly different from recipes.

(1) *Identify the problem at hand, whether from ordinary experience, how you learn, or the special or peculiar "facts and explanations" of your academic discipline.* If you are not in a condition of genuinely irritating and persistent doubt—namely, a conflict between what you may already know, or believe you already know, and that about which you wish to know—you will not even realize there is a problem to be identified. Here again is a question of our ethics of the mind: are we willing to put the consequences of our beliefs or explanations under the light of doubt? And here we must also leave open the possibility of a kind of feigned doubt, one engaged purely for the sake of some investigation.

(2) *Devise, using all the creativity you can muster, an explanation or, better still, an explanatory hypothesis (something you can* test*) that you believe might at least partially solve the problem.*

Let us take a few moments to consider this particular item rather thoroughly. The origination or selection of hypotheses Peirce termed *abduction*. Such origination, we should note, includes *guessing*. The most creative and most imaginative part of pragmatism, such abductions are also the most delicate part of pragmatic inquiry. For if we start with an irrelevant and so untestable hypothesis, we can do nothing to solve our problem or advance our knowledge. If our so-called hypothesis is not susceptible to being tested, then the search for its possible failure is impossible. This failure to specify a definite hypothesis capable of being tested Peirce called the failure to predesignate. The failure to predesignate can lead to insupportable beliefs, such as that the frequency of sunspots is a harbinger of birthrates forty weeks later. The same problem would be present should an insomniac believe that sleeplessness is inevitably produced by the nearest streetlight. In other words, without predesignation any two sets of phenomena can be imagined as functionally connected. We need more for a reliable explanation than two sets of phenomena connected in our imagination. We need to know if the connection is *real*, and for that we need predesignation, so that both confirmation and disconfirmation are possible.

Of course, such supposed cause-and-effect relations are in fact nothing but irrelevant correlations of events. Sunspots do not *cause* pregnancies; glowing streetlights do not *cause* insomnia. Predesignation requires us to form a definite, relevant, testable hypothesis or question before testing begins, but without knowing in advance how that testing will work itself out in terms of results. Predesignation, then, means that we put forward a specific "interrogation," as Peirce put it (*CP* 5.584). As you can imagine, even well-predesignated hypotheses sometimes yield only partial solutions to the problem at hand. The germ theory of disease is a good example. It is a phenomenally successful hypothetical explanation of disease, especially when compared with its predecessors, but it cannot as presently understood fully explain *all* cases of disease. Cancer and rheumatoid arthritis come to mind as disease processes that presently fall outside the group of diseases explainable by means of the germ theory. Perhaps, in time, we shall discover that these diseases too are explainable by means of the germ theory. Partial solutions at least yield partial knowledge of a given problem. They do not necessarily, in Peirce's language, "block the road of inquiry."

(3) *Carefully and assiduously test your explanation, namely your hypothesis, against that which it is alleged to explain, namely, the problem, and with just as much or more care, observe and record the results of this testing for errors.* The old bit of wisdom that *we only learn from our mistakes* applies here. If we do not take the time and *make the mistakes*, we will never have a usable method in hand which confirms that what we say we know is truly reliable knowledge, nor will the real background of our beliefs and explanations become manifest. *Without continuous testing, our knowledge remains mere suspicion.*

To repeat and expand a bit, Peirce saw pragmatism as synonymous with the experimental method of the sciences. But he did not limit this scientific method to the varieties of laboratory science associated with test tubes and microscopes, or even to formal science itself for that matter, and neither should we. Peirce saw pragmatism as the method of methods or as the method *of other methods*. It is then indeed a method of acquiring and developing human knowledge of universal scope.

In this book we shall be concerned with a study of this method of methods and of several subsidiary or adjunct methods for acquiring and developing our knowledge, rather than with a study of so-called indubitable *sources* of knowledge, which is the familiar focus of books on epistemology. We should note here that in a strict, formal sense, we do not care what the *source* of an alleged bit of knowledge may be: instead, our question is, Will this bit of knowledge survive under testing? This common denominator, this unifying and explanatory function of pragmatism, is an issue central to this book, and so a few remarks should be made, at this early point, about what "testing" can do, and what it can be the antidote to.

We live, as we all know, in an age of sometimes extreme specialization. This expresses itself in a variety of ways, not the least of which is that by the time the ordinary college or university undergraduate has completed some of his or her major course work, unspecialized conversations outside an immediate circle of fellow majors are almost impossible. Much the same is true of ordinary citizens earning their livelihoods in vocations and professions with specialized vocabularies and procedures. In the academic environment, the science-based majors come to think of the arts-based majors as students moved by and expressive of emotion, exclusively, while the arts-based majors come to think of the science-based majors as students of cold "facts" and their analyses, only. The walls between them are in place.

This same compartmentalization of various aspects of knowledge is unfortunately reflected in the academic environment at the faculty level as well, with the seemingly inevitable outcome that each specialized area of teaching and research is estranged if not divorced from most others. Many believe that this divorce is *required* because the "ways of knowing" in each discipline's area are allegedly different and incompatible. And, as you can well imagine, some "ways of knowing" are considered superior to others. Yet in spite of all the pressures that promote such divisions, the underlying distinction itself is wrong-headed.

One result of this division is that in the academic environment undergraduates receive a sort of "cafeteria style" or "scatter-shot" approach to their education: a little science here, a little literature there, a little history somewhere else, and so forth, with each discipline's offerings being implicitly estranged from all the others. A large problem looms over all of this.

Now, it is of course true that each discipline has its own vocabulary, its own facts and hypotheses. Will the facts and hypotheses of, say, the history of music in the Middle Ages prepare you for the facts and hypotheses of modern formal logic? Will the facts and hypotheses of classical mechanics prepare you for the facts and hypotheses of Mark Twain? Will the facts and hypotheses you study in any undergraduate educational or occupational environment or any other specialized course of study prepare you to handle and adapt to those groups of facts and hypotheses in your own future life that you cannot, at this moment, perhaps even imagine? Do these differing combinations of facts and hypotheses actually require completely different methods of gaining knowledge? If they do, then how well one's undergraduate education prepares one for the biggest education of all—namely *life*—will be largely a matter of luck. If you happen to hit upon just the right academic major or vocation or profession so that life unfolds in just a certain sort of way, then perhaps all will be well. Otherwise, your future competence to run your own affairs will be jeopardized. And it seems assured that if you cannot run your own affairs, then of course someone else will likely be happy to run them for you.

It is the purpose of this book to treat all these various, differing groups of facts and hypotheses under more general headings like abductive reasoning, deductive reasoning, inductive reasoning, rationalism, empiricism, dogmatism, creativity, and so forth. Each of these, in turn, is considered as a method—an adjunct of the "method of methods," which is pragmatism—for acquiring and developing human knowledge. But this by no means relegates these adjunct methods to an inferior position: each adjunct or contributing method is required to fuel the pragmatic method with the testing instruments it uses.

Let us take a few moments to consider in a general and untechnical way three of these subsidiary or adjunct methods: namely, *abductive reasoning,* by which hypotheses arise and are selected for testing; *deductive reasoning,* by which, ideally, certainty of knowledge is expressed and by which, with the finality of certainty, erroneous hypotheses are eliminated from our stocks of explanations; and *inductive reasoning,* by which, overall, probabilities are examined and according to which, for future investigations, hypotheses surviving our attempts at deductive elimination are viewed. Abductive, deductive, and inductive reasoning are intimately involved with the pragmatic, experimental process of acquiring and developing human knowledge. They define the deeper logical structure of what we may now term our pragmatic logic of events, as suggested in diagrams 1.2 and 1.3.

In due course we shall look into the technical aspects and procedures of deductive and inductive reasoning. For now, in the name of introducing the deeper architecture and logic of pragmatism, we shall examine two illustrations to give some general sense of the qualities or character of deductive and inductive procedures, following which we will take a closer look at abduction.

We all know for a practical certainty that employment of the humoral theory of disease is not going to cure anybody of anything. We also all know with a certain probability that application of the germ theory of disease and the pharmacology that has developed around it will allow us to treat successfully quite a variety of disease processes. For example, a staph infection of the foot, following second and third degree burns, may be successfully treated by intravenous administration of the antibiotic Rocefin. But some disease processes, at least at this point in the history of pathology and pharmacology, cannot be successfully treated in this manner. The common cold is a good example. Surely it is an example of an infectious disease, yet it nevertheless does not submit to treatments we now have available that are associated with the germ theory. Here again we have a hypothesis, the germ theory of disease, that yields only partial solutions.

Now, we know that the humoral theory of disease is no longer relevant in modern medicine. It *has been eliminated, with practical certainty*, from our repertoire of hypothetical explanations for disease. We know it did not perform successfully in the past, we know that even current unusual cases of disease would not be cured by its applications, and we know with practical certainty that in the future no successful application of it will ensue. We know, because it is a wrong hypothesis for the investigation of our problem, that given present knowledge there are no conceivable instances in which *it would* work. This is a general example of the kind of *practical deductive certainty* supporting human knowledge. Important for our purposes is to note that this illustration involves a *negative* kind of practical certainty: we know with practical certainty that this humoral hypothesis, given present knowledge, must be completely discarded as a possible explanation for disease *of any sort whatsoever*. It could not account *at all* for the problem at which it was directed, namely disease.

In contrast, the germ theory of disease, while extraordinarily successful as compared to the defunct humoral theory, is not in its applications always a sure bet. Sometimes the procedures we adopt based on it do indeed work, and work very well. But sometimes it does not work well at all, as with the common cold.

With the germ theory of disease we are, when dealing with new and future cases of possible application, always dealing with strong or weak *possibilities* or *probabilities*: we may be able to speak to a new or unusual case of disease with some confidence using this theory, but it must always remain a "may-be." And even when this theory works for any given case of disease we are investigating, we have no assurance that it will absolutely and without exception work in exactly the same way for all future cases even of the same disease. Microorganisms, after all, are also subject to evolution by natural selection, one result being that we now are confronted with a strain of pneumonia that is highly resistant to treatment by the antibiotics that are presently available.

With the humoral theory, we then have deductive, certain elimination of error in a practical sense; with the germ theory, we have inductive, probable success or failure in a practical sense. After discovering or selecting a hypothesis for the problem we are examining, pragmatism guides us to eliminate deductively this hypothesis, if we can. After all, even certainty of the negative sort associated with the humoral theory is still quite valuable knowledge. Pragmatism further informs us that, even with successful applications of theories like the germ theory of disease, such a theory's survival of our testing processes confers on that theory not certainty but inductive probability.

We may now consider connections between our initial Problem-Hypothesis-Test structure for knowledge and this deeper architecture and logic. If induction and probability characterize our knowledge as it moves into the future, and if deduction and certainty in either a practical or an ideal sense guide our testing of and elimination of failed hypotheses, then what characterizes the *origination* of our hypotheses? Peirce, as we know, called the invention, discovery, or selection of a hypothesis *abduction*. In lectures he gave at Harvard University in 1903, Peirce used the following description of abduction.

Abduction is the process of forming an explanatory hypothesis. It is the only logical operation which introduces any new idea; . . . [I]f we are ever to learn anything or to understand phenomena at all, it must be by abduction that this is to be brought about. No reason whatsoever can be given for it, as far as I can discover; and it needs no reason, since it merely offers suggestions. (*CP* 5.171; also Turrisi 1997: 230)

Abduction may be considered a form of reasoning in at least the sense of moving us from a state of problem-recognition and attendant doubt to the point where we have at least one supposed hypothetical solution to that doubt. In other words, it moves us from doubt to a hypothetical conclusion of that doubt, however tentative and subject to criticism and revision. If no hypothesis is brought forward to answer a problem, then obviously the PHT linkage is broken; no test can occur and no knowledge will evolve.

Many of the hypotheses we entertain in attempts to solve problems are ones we overtly select from a group of possible hypotheses. Here we use our abilities of overt, conscious reasoning. Such seems to be what we do at least in part when we work through a geometrical proof, like the one from Euclid's *Elements of Geometry* discussed earlier. There, each of the five subproblems we identified will require our selection of a suitable hypothesis from those implied or explicitly given by Euclid or perhaps provided in a commentary on Euclid. Using, for example, our third subproblem concerning the equality in length of the bases of the two given scalene triangles as an illustration of this, Euclid points us towards selecting the right hypothesis by writing "I say that the base *BC* is also equal to the base *EF*" (Euclid 1952: 4). He says to us, "Try *this!*" We are indeed guided, as beginners, toward selecting the best hypothesis for each stage of the proof. Similarly, if our automobile will not start and we are familiar generally with how automobile engines operate, then we know in advance of taking any specific corrective measures that our problem basically admits of two broad explanatory hypotheses, one dealing with fuel and the other with electricity. Given these two hypothetical options, we shall select one or both as worthy of pursuit.

The selection of a hypothesis from a list of possible explanations occurs commonly in fields as diverse as engineering, business, and law, when explanations are borrowed from solutions already successfully used elsewhere within the same subject field. Settlements of legal disputes based on precedent, on a previously successful hypothetical explanation, seem to be examples of this sort of selection. In fact, the successful selection and borrowing of hypotheses in distinct subject areas characterizes many of the major advances in human knowledge. Pasteur's understanding of the role of microorganisms in fermentation, a phenomenon well-known in the wine business, and his successful borrowing of this theory for application on disease processes is only one of many examples.

But if we commit ourselves to the idea that this sort of selection process is *the only* manner in which explanations arise for us, then we commit ourselves, even in highly ingenious borrowings, to mere repetition. And surely part of the growth of human knowledge relies on originality, on finding hypothetical explanations where none are already at hand.

The shift to the germ theory of disease seems to be an example not only of the successful selection and borrowing of a general hypothesis but also of this sort of originality. The discovery of the germ theory was of course prepared in rational, conscious ways with knowledge of fermentation, organic decay, and so forth. But *in the moment when the shift occurred, in the moment when the borrowing became a discovery*, it is difficult to find any overt, rational deliberation or conscious choice of explanation in the matter. Our focus here is on the very instant when it was seen that "This microorganism theory we have borrowed works for disease!" This sort of creative flash of insight in a moment of discovery must have also been the state of affairs for Alexander Fleming (1881–1955) when he noticed that a mold near the edge of one of his discarded culture plates was killing the plate culture of staphylococci bacteria and remarked, "That's funny" (Macfarlane 1984: 119). What Fleming had discovered in that moment was, of course, penicillin.

So abduction, whether overt, rational selection or "flash of insight," should be added to our methodical structure. Now a more complete anatomy and physiology of our pragmatic logic of events emerges, as given in diagram 1.2. Here, reading from left to right, we see where in this completed logic of events abduction and deduction have connections with the arising and initial testing of hypotheses.

Diagram 1.2

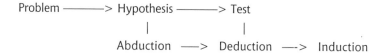

Abductive reasoning, arising in response to a Problem, yields a Hypothesis that is tested through deductive reasoning. Hypotheses not so eliminated then take on probabilistic, inductive characters.

Diagram 1.3

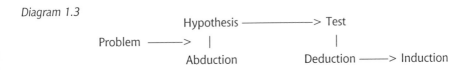

It is the filling out, the detailing and understanding of this structure describing our pragmatic logic of events that will principally concern us in the rest of this book.

In the coming pages we shall look further into how hypotheses arise abductively for our consideration and how they are subsequently appraised by deductive and, if they survive, inductive means. Not all deductive arguments reach the negative sort of conclusion that the deductive argument embedded in our appraisal of the humoral theory of disease did, and not all inductive arguments will give us the same degree of confidence about future events that the inductive argument driving our considerations of the germ theory of disease will. We shall highlight the consequences of the deductive and inductive arguments involved in the humoral and germ theories of disease toward the end of chapter 5, after we have looked at deduction, induction, and their technical aspects as subjects themselves. In contrast to deduction and induction, abduction, which is nontechnical in character, will be noted as occasions arise.

To better understand these three forms of reasoning as we proceed, we shall also consider them individually in more elaborate settings. We shall get a fuller view of the overall architecture of pragmatism, a more complete view of our pragmatic logic of events, by taking individual measures of each component part. We shall examine these component parts basically according to a pattern that begins with considerations of our common sense and the explanatory notions we routinely and constantly derive from it with abduction, and then proceed to examine rationality more generally. We shall then take up deduction, induction, and further illustrations of abduction, generally in that order. Details of all these and other topics, however, are interlaced throughout. In the last chapter we will recombine the elements of reasoning we have examined here, and we will enjoy an extraordinary application of our pragmatic logic of events, pragmatism, by the Renaissance astronomer Johannes Kepler (1571–1630). In that final chapter, we shall also take account of two serious consequences of the most creative part of the pragmatic endeavor, abduction, if it remains uncriticized. These consequences show the type of ethics of the mind necessary for the advancement of human knowledge, by contrasting it with the kind of mental ethics to be avoided. Building up the proper sort of ethics of the mind is an important consideration for us as we examine human knowledge as a subject itself.

But before proceeding, let us take a look at an ordinary example of how the basic structure of pragmatism works, and how it works in an ordinary way. Consider for a moment the building or repairing of a racing automobile. Consider the automobile in this analogy to be like an academic major, an individual academic course, the knowledge employed in a vocation or profession, or any coherent, systematic course of study. We have a variety of tools, or adjunct methods, that we can use to construct or operate such an automobile or systematic course of study. Not every tool, or adjunct method, will work for every purpose required at any given moment, though every tool will, in the long run, be used. But our ability to choose experimentally, pragmatically, between various tools and procedures, between various adjunct methods, *will* work for every circumstance we encounter. If we choose wisely and act wisely, our vehicle, for racing or for knowing, will be prepared for almost any challenge presented. If we do not so choose and *act*, neither our vehicle nor our knowledge will function, as they were intended or might have, at all.

What we find, then, in this pragmatically driven continuum of developing human knowledge are three items that, by now, should be familiar. They are:

(1) that ordinary human experience, if undogmatic, is guided, but not dictated to, by pragmatism;
(2) that every example of genuine learning is likewise guided, but not dictated to, by pragmatism;
(3) and that the progress of every academic discipline itself is guided, but not dictated to, by pragmatism.

Thus, the overall aim in the ideas contained here is to develop in the reader a heightened sense of this already-present experimental, trial-and-error, "scientific" method known as pragmatism, and to bring to the reader's notice the ethics of the mind necessary for its legitimate employment. We shall examine several additional concrete illustrations and further general indications of how it functions throughout the continuum of our knowledge.

Of necessity, then, considerable space will be given in this book to examinations of what might likely make for acceptable trials and, more importantly, to examinations of what sorts of cutting tools or filtering devices signal to us that errors are present and should be eliminated from our investigations. But no pretense is made at being exhaustive in any of these regards; this book will only begin to achieve its maximum value for any reader or course of study in which it is employed by having its general thrust actually *tested, itself,* as an hypothesis.

2

Common Sense and Learning

■ *Why not leave knowledge at common sense? The requisite and proper roles of instinct, vital topics, habits, and belief establish a foundation from which to build bridges into other areas of knowledge. Comparisons between areas of knowledge according to models and analogies aid such bridging. Self-correction as a method of inquiry is based on common sense, and our ability to detect contradictions between common sense, acquired ideas about knowledge, and the larger world improves our knowledge.*

HY BOTHER with knowledge? That is, why should any of us want to or need to "step back," from our acquisition and development of human knowledge and take a look at the actual ways and means of what we know? Put yet another way, why would we or should we wish to examine our knowledge *of* our knowledge? Why should we bother ourselves to ask a question like, Just how do I *know* that what I *say* I know really is as I say it *is*? Why additionally inquire as to the value of becoming more "objective" in these matters pertaining to our knowledge? Are not our ordinary methods of gaining knowledge, those common-sense-based apprehensions about the world around us and about ourselves as parts of that world, good enough for the conduct of many of our day-to-day affairs?

It may surprise you to learn that a satisfactory answer to this last question is an emphatic "Yes!" But it is a "yes," nevertheless, with two large qualifications. The first of these qualifications specifies or delimits just what the scope of such applications of "common sense" is, while the second takes a cautionary tone regarding applications of "common sense" beyond this stated scope. So, first, our ordinary methods of gaining and cultivating knowledge allow us to take action at times without first submitting to overt reasoning. These methods seem to work with truly remarkable success and consistency when applied to those subjects and issues in life that Peirce ironically called "Vitally Important Topics." One such vitally important topic is our instinct to survive, and the "unreasoned" actions we associate with this topic consist in those well-settled habits of belief and action that express this instinctual drive. Note that *unreasoned* does not mean the same thing as *unreasonable*.

A second, cautionary qualification consists in the mere acknowledgment that there is, quite obviously, an enormous realm of human knowledge beyond such vital topics where reactively and exclusively using such ordinary, unreasoned methods can get us into serious, and sometimes intractable, difficulties. That is to say, such ordinary methods of gaining and developing human knowledge can be frightfully misapplied. Pitiable situations come to mind, like those that have unfolded with such groups as the followers of the Reverend Jim Jones who, at their leader's bidding, committed suicide in the Guyanan jungle, and the disciples of David Koresh who, following their "family" leader, died in their farm house rather than surrending to the FBI. It would seem that in playing on the fears of their followers—and in inviting their followers to act on these fears in unreasoned, *seemingly* commonsensical sorts of ways—these two individuals cost hundreds of people their very lives. And do not suppose that we are singling out, in these regards, examples concerned with religion in general or with Christianity in particular. Charles Keating and his savings-and-loan swindles would work just as well as illustrations of "common sense misapplied" and "common sense led astray." Nor should you suppose that we are deliberately targeting cases involving the mere superficial appearance of religion, although it seems to me that the superficiality of such cases as these involving Jones and Koresh illustrates rather devastatingly how unreasoned "common sense" can dangerously, even fatally, be manipulated.

This relationship between the unreasoned realm of vital topics and its larger companion can be diagrammed for greater ease of inspection, as in diagram 2.1. Here we use a graphical, diagrammatic technique borrowed from the noted eighteenth-century mathematician Leonhard Euler, modified so that only the relative sizes of the two sets or collections of things are illustrated by rectangles of corresponding size.

Also included here is a cue from a certain development in nineteenth-century mathematics known as topology. Thus, the following diagrammatic expression of the relation between the two sets of knowledge items labeled as "Vitally Important Topics" and, for lack of a better phrase at present, "All the Rest" depends not on the precisely measurable sizes of the rectangles selected, but rather on their *relative* sizes and positions: the one rectangle smaller than the other, the smaller rectangle enclosed within the larger one. According to the principles of topology, this relation would remain even should the diagram as a whole be "stretched" or otherwise deformed.

And this is a diagram upon which we may perform various experiments, graphically recording our efforts at each step along the way. Note that, just as this diagram visually demonstrates, the area of human knowledge concerned with such vitally important topics seems smaller than, and somehow different from, our knowledge as a whole.

Diagram 2.1

all the rest

Vitally Important Topics

This seems in fact to be the case in life, that some portions of our lives are moved along in what appear to be decidedly unreasoned ways, while that larger arena of belief and action demands of us a method or methods of acquiring and developing our knowledge that exceeds, but could be based on, our common-sense-based, unreasoned, vitally important procedures.

"But," you ask, "how can we have really 'unreasoned' knowledge, and if we do in fact possess such an odd-seeming variety of knowledge, what warrant or guarantee do we have that we can really *trust* in it?" This is as important a pairing of questions, on the issue of how we know that we really *do* know, as can be asked, and it invites experimentation with our initial diagram.

Responding to the invitation to experiment, how can we improve our diagram to better represent our actual states of affairs, vis-à-vis knowledge? We can begin by clarifying the language to make the diagram more easily understood for general purposes.

Diagram 2.2

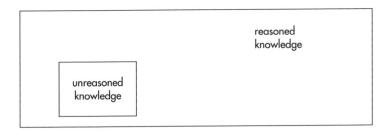

As before, please note the differences in the relative sizes of the two rectangles used. This difference is meant to convey the notion that, on a purely quantitative level, unreasoned knowledge seems to play the relatively minor role. In terms of accurately portraying these two categories of our knowledge, this diagram is an improvement on its predecessor.

Now that the purpose for these different sized rectangles is a bit clearer, and given that our adoption of simpler and plainer descriptions of their contents has likewise had a beneficial effect, we must further ask about the completeness of our diagram. Is it complete? Are there any subcategories or subcompartments to be found in either rectangle? It seems that indeed there are.

The collection or set of knowledge items labeled "unreasoned" knowledge might be further divided into two parts. Both of these parts deal with our instincts. The word *instincts* might very well produce the following response: "Instincts? I thought that we, as human beings, were supposed to have disciplined ourselves to avoid or suppress mere *instincts*! Instincts are what move the *lower* animals, and surely we are better than the lower animals!" But instinct is, after all, important for human beings as well. Leaving aside for the moment all judgments of "better or worse," consider that we all operate, at that common-sense level of unreasoned knowledge, with two different, but intimately connected, sets of instincts. One set is what can be termed "inborn instincts"—what we are all apparently born with. The other amounts to what we all practice as "acquired instincts"—what experience teaches each of us to employ or reject. But we cannot ignore either variety of instinct for very long.

Consider again, for a moment, the survival function of our undoubtedly inborn or innate instinct. The most cursory visit to a hospital will demonstrate, sometimes in disturbing ways, just how strong this instinct really is. All of us are familiar with examples of persons in real medical danger who, somehow, continue to survive; consider for a moment the heroic struggles of premature infants. Are these persons *taught* that they must do their best to survive? Did their parents take them aside shortly after birth and render instruction in the matter? Of course not. The basic genetic and biological will to live, in such cases as these, is present, already, at birth. To make plain the point, there is not, in such cases as these, *any* reasoning involved that produces the required knowledge for survival. Peirce provided an interesting observation on these issues in the first of his 1898 Cambridge Conferences Lectures, "Philosophy and the Conduct of Life":

But, in practical affairs, in matters of Vital Importance, it is very easy to exaggerate the importance of ratiocination [to reason methodically and logically]. Man is so vain of his power of reason! It seems impossible for him to see himself in this respect, as he himself would see himself if he could duplicate himself and observe himself with a critical eye. Those whom we are so fond of referring to as the "lower animals" reason very little. Now I beg you to observe that those beings very rarely commit a *mistake*, while we ———! We employ twelve good men and true to decide a question, we lay the facts before them with the greatest care, the "perfection of human reason" presides over the presentment, they hear, they go out and deliberate, they come to a unanimous opinion, and it is generally admitted that the parties to the suit might almost as well have tossed up a penny to decide! Such is man's glory! The mental qualities we most admire in all human beings except our several selves are the maiden's delicacy, the mother's devotion, manly courage, and other inheritances that have come to us from the biped who did not yet speak; while the characters that are most contemptible take their origin in reasoning. The very fact that everybody so ridiculously overrates his own reasoning, is sufficient to show how superficial the faculty is. For you do not hear the courageous man vaunt his own courage, or the modest woman boast of her modesty, or the really loyal plume themselves on their honesty. What they *are* vain about is always some insignificant gift of beauty or of skills.

It is the instincts, the sentiments, that make the substance of the soul. Cognition is only its surface, its locus of contact with what is external to it. (Peirce 1898, MS 437: 11–12; *RLT*: 110)

So it looks like we would be wise to adopt provisionally the idea that "unreasoned knowledge" somehow includes such innate or inborn knowledge. What about "acquired instincts?" What might these be? Will they find a place in our diagram?

What do you take to be an ordinary, person-in-the-street understanding of instinct? Most people will say that instinct, so considered, involves some sort of involuntary, automatic response or action that nevertheless differs from neurological *reflex*. This understanding comports rather well with the idea that some instincts, and their accompanying knowledge items, are innate or inborn in all of us. But what about this proposal of mine that there might be a collection or set of learned or "acquired" instincts, complete with another set of accompanying knowledge items? You will ask, "How can anything *learned* be squared or made agreeable with this automatic-seeming nature of *instinct?*"

Whenever we enter into the relation between ourselves and some subject matter that eventually results in knowledge of that subject, we at first feel a definite conflict between what we already think we know and this new-seeming subject we are about to learn. This conflict can be described as "doubt." This is but another means for reiterating and reexamining the shopworn maxim that, in learning of practically any sort, we do indeed work from what we know to what we do not quite yet know. In other words, we take what we have accepted as true, what we *believe* in a fixed way, and proceed to compare or test such "fixed beliefs" against challenges to them. Now such fixed beliefs are also called "knowledge." Beyond the realm of innate or inborn ideas, this "knowledge" also goes by our still-awkward and seemingly paradoxical phrase "acquired instincts." A better name may now be introduced, namely, habits. Ponder that word, *habits*, for a moment. Even the most ordinary understanding of the term includes two features useful to our present investigations of how we proceed from the already-known to the eventually-to-be-known and how unreasoned common sense, absolutely invaluable as a starting point in the process of learning or acquiring knowledge, must eventually be supplemented and accompanied by reasoned efforts and results. These two features of habits are (1) that they seem to have much of that involuntary or automatic character we usually associate with innate or inborn instincts, ideas, or knowledge and (2) that they can be changed or modified.

Habit here means something much broader than my own propensity to smoke cigarettes, but this will serve as a good, already-known starting point. After many years of practice, my desire for a cigarette with my morning coffee is almost unconscious, certainly unreasoned, and some combination of involuntary and automatic action. In this respect, this habit of smoking quite resembles an inborn instinct. But unlike a truly inborn instinct, that is, an instinct like survival that is driven and regulated by our genetic codes and their interplay with our surrounding and enwrapping environment, this habit of smoking can be changed or modified.

This line of reasoning all goes to a much deeper level of knowledge, belief, truth, doubt, and habit than may at first be obvious. It leads us to a level of primitive knowledge that deals in quite immediate ways with what we think we know. In my own case, my smoking habit expresses the apparent belief that smoking is harmless. At this level I ask myself, "Can I take this apparent belief as something true, or is this belief false, or should I suspend my own potentially egoistic judgment, my disbelief, until I truly understand this situation with smoking or until more convincing evidence appears?" Yet this level of primitive knowledge conflicts with my habitual behavior. The history of the matter reveals that I take the view that "smoking is harmless" as true. Is that not the knowledge-item characterization of my habit, a truth claim that I apparently do not doubt, a well-fixed belief on my part?

Hypothetically, what might encourage me to stop smoking, to modify my habit toward a truer and more accurate, but equally habitual, belief? Perhaps a disastrous medical examination would do it. Perhaps a vivid recollection of a trusted and valued friend who died from lung cancer shortly after exhibiting symptoms alarmingly like my own. In other words, the world around me might present arresting evidence that my belief, what I think I know and for a certainty, is *erroneous*. Put another way, in the face of such evidence I become afraid. Doubt arises. The resolution of such doubt entails our acknowledgment of real world, one with which we try to align our beliefs. Peirce described such alignment of beliefs with their corresponding realities as "self-control" (*CP* 5.130; 5.420).

The passage from fixed beliefs, habits, or presumed "already-knowns" to these conditions of doubt produced by a disagreement between our fixed beliefs and those very things *about* which our beliefs are fixed, is part of what we call learning. Learning is also that process that moves us to and through doubt toward the acquisition and development of human knowledge. It is important to note that the actions of habits, when thoroughly fixed, do not seem to proceed from any reasoning. But the alleviation of doubt that brings about newly fixed beliefs or habits, the same process that helps us get at the truths of the world around us, *does* entail reasoning. Based on these observations, we may devise another experimental improvement in our diagram. Please note here that *reasonable*, which implies a kind of capacity or potential, does not mean the same thing as *reasoned*, which means that this capacity or potential has been realized or brought into play.

Diagram 2.3

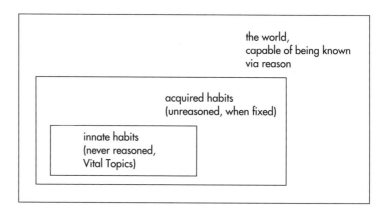

For the sake of simplicity, let us narrow our field of inspection here, somewhat. At the risk of oversimplicity, let us abbreviate the residents of these realms as "Our Habits" and "The World." Where they meet is where our knowledge forms, given in diagram 2.4 as a question mark indicating the uncertainty and fallible nature of the interchange between our habits and our environment.

Diagram 2.4

Our Habits <———-> ? <———-> The World

Now what, exactly, are the functions of habits in this diagrammatic representation? Basically, we find habits playing one of three roles. First, they may have no contact with the world at all, or, perhaps worse, they may share a kind of twisted relationship with it, thus producing such things as general narrow-mindedness, dogmatism, bigotry, even schizophrenia. In other words, when habits have no real contact with the world, no learning takes place and our so-called knowledge can never be confirmed as anything more than a mere suspicion.

When habits do have contact with the world around them—a world of which they are themselves a part—the second and third options become available. The second option finds habits at such loggerheads with the world that a truly fundamental question about our knowledge presents itself, and it can present itself in rather devastating ways. Thus, when our habits, beliefs, knowledge-items, explanations, hypotheses, and theories conflict with the very world they are supposed to make plain to us and when we find after suitable efforts that our habits *cannot* adapt themselves to the world, which of the two must go: our habits or the world? Which of the two can we change?

The third option finds habits pursuing the process of self-correcting doubt, "self-control," in a truly experimental fashion, by which we modify or discard erroneous habits and retain successful habits in our knowledge for further comparison with the world. (This, by the way, is a short but reliable description of pragmatism.) Referring back to diagrams 2.3 and 2.4 and their illustrations of the relationship between habits and the world, we find that such "successful" or "surviving" habits move us toward a larger understanding of the world. As our knowledge increases, the size of the rectangle for habits likewise increases. As this process works, you might visualize it as portions of the world being absorbed into our habit-realm. But when this absorption occurs, what exactly gets "absorbed" and how does this occur? This is a question of primary importance.

To grasp its importance, consider the following extract from one of Peirce's 1906 "Pragmatism" essays proposed for *The Nation*. Note carefully his remarks about our inner and outer worlds, the acquisition of habits, and especially his description of the burning dress. What, exactly, had his brother Herbert learned that allowed him to act so decisively and beneficially?

Every sane person lives in a double world, the outer and the inner world, the world of percepts and the world of fancies. Habits differ from dispositions in having been acquired as consequences of the principle, virtually well-known even to those whose powers of reflexion are insufficient to its formulation, that multiple reiterated behaviour of the same kind, under similar combinations of percepts and fancies, produces a tendency—the *habit*—actually to behave in a similar way under similar circumstances in the future. Moreover—*here is the point*—every man exercises more or less control over himself by means of modifying his own habits; and the way in which he goes to work to bring this effect about in those cases in which circumstances will not permit him to practice reiterations of the desired kind of conduct in the outer world shows that he is virtually well-acquainted with the important principle that *reiterations in the inner world—fancied reiterations—if well-intensified by direct effort, produce habits,* just as do reiterations in the outer world; *and these habits will have power to influence actual behaviour in the outer world;* especially, if each reiteration be accompanied by a peculiar strong effort that is usually likened to issuing a command to one's future self. [A note, thereafter, follows below.]

I well remember when I was a boy, and my brother Herbert, now our minister at Christiania, was scarce more than a child, one day, as the whole family were at table, some spirit from a "blazer," or "chafing-dish," dropped on the muslin dress of one of the ladies [their mother] and was kindled; and how instantaneously he jumped up, and did the right thing [smothered the fire with a rug], and how skillfully each motion was adapted to the purpose. I asked him afterward about it; and he told me that since Mrs. Longfellow's death, it was that he had often run over in imagination all the details of what ought to be done in such an emergency. It was a striking example of a real habit produced by exercises in the imagination. (CP 5.487)

The Mrs. Longfellow mentioned toward the end of this extended quotation was Fanny Appleton Longfellow, second wife of the poet William Wadsworth Longfellow, who died on 10 July 1860 from burns received the prior day when the summer dress she was wearing caught fire from a dropped match (Williams 1964: 91). What had Herbert absorbed and how did this absorption occur? Had he literally taken in the experience of Mrs. Longfellow's death? Of course not. In fact, the record does not indicate that any of the Peirces were present at Mrs. Longfellow's accident; so when Charles writes of his brother Herbert's actions as "a striking example of a real habit produced by exercises in the imagination," he means literally exercises practiced *only* in imagination. Was his response to the emergency based on acquired habits divorced from the world? Again, surely not. Was some innate-seeming habit, like the bond between parent and child, involved? To some extent, surely yes.

This example should strike us as one rather representative of just what goes on when we acquire knowledge *in general*. When Herbert Peirce saw his mother's dress on fire, it seems that three factors determined his knowledge of what to do in response to the situation.

First, he felt some sort of innate, habitual empathy towards his fellow human beings. This made him receptive to the previous experience involving Mrs. Longfellow, from which he learned, *in her particular instance*, what should be done. That is, he did not come to the experience of that woman's death devoid of previous cognitions that might have some bearing on her situation. So, with the "knowledge baggage" that he brought to Mrs. Longfellow's experience, plus his second-hand knowledge of the phenomenon itself, he began to suspect that perhaps there was more to Mrs. Longfellow's circumstance than an explanation of it as an absolutely isolated incident could provide.

Second, through "exercises in the imagination" he began to understand that, perhaps, somewhere within all this there just might be a general maxim of action applicable to his "future self." He then produced for himself an acquired habit, that is, he learned what should be done.

Third, he saw his mother's dress on fire and, equipped with the appropriate acquired habit, he acted.

Now let us pick a typical academic subject and see if this "belief-doubt-belief" model of acquiring and developing knowledge, suggested by Peirce, actually works. If it does, it should help to answer our questions about what, fundamentally, gets absorbed when we learn something new, and how we carry what we absorb into new regions of knowledge.

Let us suppose that we are intent on learning a new level of mathematics, one we have not been exposed to before. What happens? Just like Herbert Peirce we first come to this new and unfamiliar subject with a certain set of habits already in place, habits in math, let us call them. We wish to learn geometry, in particular Euclidean geometry at the level taken up in our first chapter. Arithmetic would be the subject of our already-present habit, our "belief in our already-known."

Diagram 2.5

The World of
Eventually-To-Be-Knowns
(geometry)

Habits, Beliefs
already in place
(arithmetic)

In Herbert's case it appeared that some actual innate habits might be involved at the beginning of the process. We would probably be reluctant to claim that we have actual innate habits specially fitted for the study of mathematics, but this is really beside the point for the moment. The overall issue is the same in the cases of both Herbert Peirce and us, namely, we do not come to new experiences of knowledge completely devoid of previous experiences that will, in one way or another, have a bearing on our new experiences. To paraphrase Peirce, there is no such thing as an absolutely *first cognition*.

Second, analogous to Herbert, we are confronted with a new experience, which is, in our case, geometry. Doubt and the lure of the eventually-to-be-known enter our processes of acquiring and developing knowledge. By manipulation of and experimentation on both imaginary and visual diagrams that make plain our various hypothetical attempts to explain problems, in our particular case diagrams both imaginary and visual, and by the careful observation and correction of our diagrams, we come to a new condition of fixed belief with its companion acquired habit. We have learned something of geometry.

Third, based on this newly acquired habit, we are prepared to act in future situations involving an understanding of geometry. It is important to note here, in conjunction with diagram 2.5, that geometry now comes to reside in the lower left-hand part of the diagram. It may now be used as a "previous cognition" for further mathematical pursuits.

But still the question remains: At the most fundamental level of human knowledge, what do we absorb when we learn something new? And here we mean *LEARN* rather than mechanically reproduce the peculiarities of vocabulary and subject matter that distinguish academic disciplines, professions, and vocations. Better yet, what *equips* us to absorb new and unfamiliar knowledge? What is it that allows us to proceed from the known to the unknown?

As with the dramatic event in the life of Herbert Peirce, as with geometry, as with everything else we count as knowledge, those things that we absorb anew every time we learn, those things that equip us to absorb anew in the first place, and every time, are certain fundamental, analogically employed *principles* or adjunct *elements* of knowledge falling under our pragmatic rubric. These elemental principles that underlie knowledge acquisition are three in number, each one composed of a pair of seemingly opposed notions about human knowledge that have always vexed us in the past and still vex us today. They can be phrased in three questions that deal with the subjects of process and evidence.

(1) Is deriving our knowledge a process yielding absolute *certainty*, or is it a process yielding relative *probability*?

(2) In deriving our knowledge, do we or should we depend more often or even exclusively on evidence having an objective or creative character, or should we rely only on apparent evidence produced by our own *subjective* or *dogmatic* considerations?

(3) In deriving our knowledge, do we or should we employ fixed, *rote* procedures, or should we depend on experimental, *pragmatic* ones?

Herbert Peirce imagined, learned, and established a new habit and acted upon it because of some rather exact structural similarities between the case of Mrs. Longfellow and that of his own mother. In other words, for Herbert Peirce the similarity between the cases of the unseen Mrs. Longfellow and the clearly seen Mrs. Peirce were so exact, so duplicative of one another as to function as actual structural *models* of one another. Surely, from our standpoint, we would consider Herbert Peirce's experiments in his imagination as pragmatic, probabilistic, creative acts resulting in an objectively observable result.

In such exact cases as Herbert Peirce compared, little must be learned anew in any successive application of the model itself, alone. True, subject matters themselves change as we move into more advanced and complicated areas, but a move to any other structural model of the same type does not likewise involve further complication beyond that of the subject matter itself. That is why we can proceed from arithmetic to geometry—because we observe and build on certain structural similarities. But we proceed in this mathematical example according to certain looser, more creative similarities or *analogies*. Structuring analogies is the process that, given the existence and actions of microorganisms like bacteria, informs the move from studies of fermentation to observations of organic decay to the germ theory of disease. Peirce gave a definition of "analogy" in the original edition of W. D. Whitney's *Century Dictionary* that illustrates this meaning of the term. Here is a relevant part.

Analogy strictly denotes only a partial similarity, as in some special circumstances of effects predictable of two or more things in other respects essentially different: thus, when we say that learning *enlightens* the mind, we recognize an *analogy* between learning and light, the former being to the mind what the latter is to the eye, enabling it to discover things before hidden. We say that there is an analogy *between* things. (Peirce 1889: 195)

In this sort of learning process, then, we say to ourselves, "In certain respects, what I already know is either a structural model of or an analogy of what I wish to know, and upon these similarities I can build a bridge to further my investigation of this new area."

How is it that we can move among a variety of vocabularies and subject matters, however wildly they may seem to be different? We know that the average U.S. citizen will change types of employment several times over a working career, that members of professions take time to update their competencies, and that academics place a good deal of emphasis on creative endeavors that advance knowledge in their fields—clearly we *do* make such moves. How is it that college or university students learn subjects as diverse and apparently different from one another as fine arts and laboratory sciences? Such simultaneous learning can take place because, just as in the cases of Herbert Peirce and our learning of geometry, certain elemental structural principles or models and analogies underlie, it seems, *any and all* of our acquisitions and developments of human knowledge. Some such cases, like the one of Herbert Peirce, depend on similarities so exact and so strong as to be actual structural *models* of one another. Others, like moving from fermentation to the germ theory or moving from arithmetic to geometry, function rather more like examples of the looser, less strict type of structural similarity denoted by *analogy*. Understanding these principles of learning will help you to apply them not only within an academic setting but also within the conduct of life in general, to make the acquisition of knowledge in any area more thorough and systematic, and smoothen the whole learning process.

It is important to recognize that the three principles mentioned above organize not only the various subjects and disciplines themselves that we encounter, the *what* of what we know, but also the processes by which we come to learn these subjects and disciplines, the *how* of what we know. Discovering how to get the best pairing of *what* with *how* in any given learning situation is the key.

These three questions concerning certainty and probability, objectivity and creativity, and rote versus experimental approaches form the backdrop for the topics associated with the pragmatic acquisition and development of human knowledge that we examine here. Among our adjunct methods certain ones will be found that enable us to realize a number of improvable goals desirable for our mental ethics. Thus, deductive reasoning can bring us certain truth, while inductive reasoning can bring us probability, strong or weak. Critical creativity supplies the road to objectivity, but dogmatism and subjectivity only appear to feed off one another. Likewise, the rote procedures and unreflective repetitions inherent in the dogmatic and the subjectivistic approaches are found to be anathema to genuine, evolutionary progress in our knowledge. Similarly, Peirce's method of pragmatism, which can be summarized as the experimental method of all these adjunct methods, forms the umbrella under which all these and other adjunct methods are considered. Pragmatism provides an over-arching rationale and method for selecting among the various types and combinations of adjunct methods available, and it also supplies an experimental, self-correcting technique for evaluating their consequences.

3

Rationality and Argument

■ *Self-criticism is based on principles of rationality. Although irrationality is to be avoided, both rationality and nonrationality have clear roles to play in the acquisition and development of knowledge. Argument assists in determining which claims for knowledge are objective or subjective. An illustration from the Bible shows how the Philippian jailer acts upon a formal argument, but a formal argument defective in informal ways.*

*T*HERE ARE, of course, a variety of methods for acquiring and developing knowledge and methods of fixing belief in a given subject area. We employ these methods regularly, whether to determine courses of action in our everyday lives or to learn about and attempt to master academic pursuits. Unsurprisingly, these methods vary in their effectiveness. Let us try to determine, from a commonsense point of view, what sort of fixation of belief would strike us, in any given situation, as the best.

Let us suppose that the issue about which we wish to learn and, eventually, adopt a course of action is a perceived need for heart surgery. What sorts of factors would figure intelligently in making a decision about such a perceived need? Undoubtedly, such factors as the opinions of one's regular physician and of the consulted cardiologist would play a major role in coming to a decision in this matter. Now, why should these opinions weigh so heavily in making a decision about heart surgery? One would likely prefer the advice of such experts over other forms and expressions of opinion because these persons have reached their conclusion, their advice to you, not on the basis of uninformed opinion but as a result of genuine argument. What is meant by *argument*, in this sense?

An argument, in its most basic sense, is a process by which a claim is made about something and, more importantly, is backed up or supported by relevant evidence organized in a persuasive manner. The claim in our situation is the conclusion reached by the consulted physicians that heart surgery is called for. The evidence presented, in this case, could take several forms, among which might be a medical history of steadily declining heart function, a genetic history of similar difficulties, clearly disturbing results obtained from uses of electrocardiography and angiography, and the like. In contrast, noting how much it has rained today or who is currently the president of the United States or whether the local trees have budded would not be useful evidence in this matter. Similarly, if someone used your medical history and coronary symptoms as justification for the notion that he should be crowned the King of Spain, we would, likewise, be suspicious of the employed "evidence." Of course, if parallel tracks for these medical and monarchial phenomena were claimed over a period of time with alleged cause and effect relations between events in them, we would again be confronted, as we were in chapter 1, with what Peirce called failures to predesignate. The lack of definite, testable hypotheses leads to such faulty connections of irrelevant events. But not only are we again seeing the fruits of failing to predesignate; both examples should also alert us to another, equally severe problem, namely, that the process of *reasoning*—the process that should link relevant evidence to a relevant conclusion—is also defective. The so-called "evidence," empirically derived, and the powers of human reason combine here to produce conclusions that are nonsense.

To summarize these matters, let us reconfigure our description of an argument to produce something a bit more tidy. Thus, an argument is a process in which a *conclusion* claimed as true or false is supported by relevant evidence in the form of a *premise*, and the connection between premise (or premises) and conclusion is one governed by the best possible *reasoning*.

So, we accept the opinion and advice of our medical experts because their opinion and advice is the result of adequate predesignation and argument rather than the product of, say, superstition or mere personal or subjective feeling. Please notice that this use of "argument" is very different from the sorts of shouting matches we often associate with that term. The kind of argument we are interested in with our surgery illustration produces, unlike the subjective shouting match variety, a conclusion that is *objective*—which means that, although discovered by human minds and human reason, it is independent of us, or real. Given investigators who can understand the issues involved and who do not have a private, prearranged agenda to follow, the same evidence and the same reasoning should consistently lead to the same conclusion, regardless of which investigators are involved. Such objective results are conclusions that command the respect of all competent observers, rather like the notion in classical mechanics that objects dropped near the surface of the earth will fall, if unimpeded, at a rate of acceleration of 32 ft./sec./sec. Our mere subjective opinions or feelings in the matter are completely irrelevant. In fact, the phenomenon of acceleration would function just the same without any human observers to note it at all. Such objective conclusions or knowledge-items are like a collection of materials or objects placed on a writing desk: they are "there," available for all to see. Mere subjective squabbling, while it may produce a satisfying consensus or a unanimity of opinion, will not, in and of itself, produce knowledge about issues that have an objective character.

You may recall that civilized people, for a time, formed a strong consensus as to what should be done with individuals whom they characterized as witches. The way they treated alleged witches can illustrate what are known as informal fallacies in reasoning. *Fallacy* means *error*, both in the sense of a mistake having been made and in the sense of failure in our reasoning processes. The failure to predesignate, for example, is one such fallacy. By comparison, "formal fallacies," which we will take up in chapter 5, are violations of the logical limits of a standardized form or pattern of deductive reasoning: as in the argument all human beings are mammals; all dogs are mammals; therefore, all human beings are dogs.

Informal fallacies, however, concern basic questions about the relevance of the evidence offered in support of some conclusion. Thus, in the case of witches, a serious problem confronts the investigator trying to find relevant evidence to support the conclusion that witches exist or the opposite conclusion that they do not exist. One can well imagine an exchange like the following between two people arguing over this question. Arguer A: "Well, it's a certainty that there *are* witches, because nobody has ever proven that there *aren't* any!" Arguer B: "Nonsense! Of course there are no such things as witches, because nobody has ever proven that there *are* such things as witches!"

The difficulty in this *argument from ignorance*, as this informal fallacy is termed, is that each arguer cites in favor of his conclusion the fact that no convincing evidence for the opposite conclusion has been put forward. But none could be! The same circumstance arises with arguments over claims made by parapsychology and astrology. It is tempting to think that this fallacy should be termed "argument from *enforced* or *unavoidable* ignorance," because the existence of witches and many of the claims of parapsychologists and astrologists are matters outside the bounds of objective testing procedures. As such, they are not matters, as yet at least, that can guide us to an objective point of view: they are not objective matters dealing with objective evidence. Recalling the irrelevant correlation of sunspots and pregnancies (a failure to predesignate) that we noted in chapter 1, we can detect the relationship between failure to predesignate and an argument from ignorance. In short, it appears that all arguments from ignorance are by default instances of failures to predesignate. But, using the example connecting sunspots and pregnancies as an illustration, not all failures to predesignate are arguments from ignorance. We are not, in the correlation between sunspots and pregnancies, drawing a conclusion based on hopeless, unavoidable ignorance. Sunspots and pregnancies and alleged relations between them are things about which we *can* have objective knowledge.

Objective matters, then, are matters about which all informed and reasonable persons should, eventually, agree. The histories of various inquiries, such as the history of medical pathology, disclose this tendency, especially when errors and misconceptions arise and must be eliminated or corrected.

All this can be phrased in a different and more compelling manner. When we reach such objective conclusions, we have conducted ourselves according to the dictates of being creatures who are *rational*. That is, we try, whenever possible in such matters, to use relevant types and sufficient amounts of evidence, to draw conclusions consistent with the evidence and to draw such conclusions in just that way because we have used good reasoning.

For example, if I have a well-fixed belief that I can hop into my red sports car and drive from this location to a nearby city, this is surely a rational belief on my part. When I say that I know that I can do this (or, to get a bit technical about it, when I say, "The statement 'Stewart can drive to a nearby city' is true"), I have fixed my belief in a rational manner. Thus, the relevant statement, "Stewart can drive to a nearby city," is my conclusion; the premises consist in the existence of the proper equipment, pavement, abilities, and a past history along these lines; and the good reasoning consists in the fact that, combining all the pieces of evidence and putting them into play, it is perfectly reasonable to presume that the conclusion will result. Whether or not such a conclusion is a matter of absolute certainty or relative probability is an important question that will, shortly, command our attention.

If, on the other hand, I have a well-fixed belief that, by flapping my arms furiously and launching myself from the roof of the local bank, I can *fly* to a nearby city, then I am most assuredly operating in an *irrational* manner. How long I can continue to operate with this belief is a question that could be answered by purely empirical means, by my attempt to fly after leaping from the bank roof. Similar means might have been employed, pragmatically rather than dogmatically, by those who believed in witchery. These cases are worth study because they illustrate the danger of irrationality and of blindly following important-sounding advice, thereby convincing ourselves that some mechanistic, dogmatic approach to knowledge will provide us with a guarantee that our knowledge or beliefs are assured and insured. In his "Our Senses as Reasoning Machines" of 1900, Peirce gave a summation of this problem:

> What, then, is the use of designating some formations of opinion as rational, while others (perhaps leading to the same results) are stigmatized as blind following of the rule of thumb or of authority, or as mere guesses? When we reason, we set out from an assumed representation of a state of things. This we call our *premise*; and working upon this, we produce another representation that professes to refer to the same state of things; and this we call our *conclusion*. But so we do when we go irreflectively by a rule of thumb, as when we apply a rule of arithmetic the reason of which we have never been taught. The irrationality here consists in our following a fixed method, of the correctness of which the other method affords no assurance; so that if it does not happen to be right in its application to the case at hand, we go hopelessly astray. In genuine reasoning, we are not wedded to our method. We deliberately approve it, but we stand ever ready and disposed to reexamine it and to improve upon it, and to criticize our criticism of it, without cessation (Peirce 1900, MS 831: 9–11).

We can conclude then that irrationality—whether from an immediate and abrupt conflict with good reasoning and the facts of the world or brought on more gradually by operating from an ignorantly followed or dogmatically held method—cannot produce objective knowledge or reliable fixations of belief. In the arm-flapping flight illustration, above, the principal fault seems to derive from my defective reasoning having led me to embrace an inaccurate, if not outright false, picture of the world around me and how it ordinarily operates.

If choosing appropriate subsidiary methods is part of our pragmatic business too, then we see that irrationality characterizes such mischoosings as thinking the Black Death of fourteenth century Europe and Asia due to divine retribution. So, rational behavior involves good reasoning while irrational behavior involves bad reasoning. Both the actual, immediately experienced consequences and the imaginable practical consequences of using acceptable or defective reasoning can help us improve reasoning that is a bit weak, or else lead us to discard reasoning that is plainly wrong.

There is yet another realm in which human knowledge and belief are conspicuous, a realm that seems set apart from both the rational and irrational. This is the realm of the *nonrational*. If rationality implies good reasoning while irrationality implies bad reasoning, then nonrationality seems to leave reasoning out of the acquisition and development of human knowledge altogether. How could knowledge or the fixation of belief occur in the complete absence of reasoning? That is, how could we be confident in making claims that are not supported at all by reasoning, whether that reasoning be good or bad? What sorts of topics or subjects could be approached by a nonrational means? The answer to this last question may lead us to an understanding of how nonrational insight and subsequent critical knowledge can come about.

Rationality depends on good reasoning and produces knowledge, in most matters. Irrationality stems from poor reasoning and can yield lunacy, if not criticized. Nonrationality offers no reasoning at all and produces results that, for the long run, cannot be relied upon without criticism.

An example of nonrationality is instinct. Obviously, our previous examination of inherited instinct clearly shows any instance of such truly instinctual knowledge to be nonrational in nature: we do not reason about it and probably are not even clearly aware of it. But bear in mind that with such truly inborn knowledge, no learning or acquisition seems to have taken place. One does not, *in utero*, methodically calculate whether or not the drive to survive is a good thing to cultivate or a rationally derived thing to believe. This example of inborn instinct is not of much interest to us at the present. What is of interest to us are any possible candidates for nonrational belief that do actually involve and produce acquired knowledge.

In the remainder of this chapter I will put forward three subjects that seem clearly to involve nonrational insight or fixation of belief in such an acquisitive manner. They involve genuine religious experience, private emotional states like falling in (or out of) love, and profound moments when an "aha!" or flash experience of artistic comprehension occurs. We are not concerned, for the moment, about the sorts of theological or pseudo-theological debates that can precede or follow upon authentic religious experiences, or about the rationalizations that often accompany our truly transitional emotional states, or about critical and reflective assessments that sometimes lead up to and follow after moments of real, legitimate artistic enlightenment. What is of interest here are those "moments of truth" inherent in each of these three cases, those particular, singular instances of religious, emotional, and artistic immediacy that overwhelm us, that so thoroughly saturate our cognitive processes that during those moments the possibility of rational consideration is totally obscured.

One such instance, dealing with the religious variety of acquired, nonrational insight, is recorded in chapter 16 of the New Testament's Acts of the Apostles: verses 25–34 generally and verses 30–31 in particular. This is the account of the conversion of the Philippian jailer, a striking instance of such a singular moment.

And at midnight Paul and Silas prayed, and sang praises unto God: and the prisoners heard them. [26] And suddenly there was a great earthquake, so that the foundations of the prison were shaken: and immediately all the doors were opened, and every one's bands were loosed. [27] And the keeper of the prison awaking out of his sleep, and seeing the prison-doors open, he drew out his sword, and would have killed himself, supposing that the prisoners had been fled. 28 But Paul cried with a loud voice, saying, Do thyself no harm: for we are all here. 29 Then he called for a light, and sprang in, and came trembling, and fell down before Paul and Silas; 30 And brought them out, and said, Sirs, what must I do to be saved? 31 And they said, Believe on the Lord Jesus Christ, and thou shalt be saved, and thy house. 32 And they spake unto him the word of the Lord, and to all that were in his house. 33 And he took them the same hour of the night, and washed their stripes; and was baptized, he and all his, straightway. 34 And when he had brought them into his house, he set meat before them, and rejoiced, believing in God with all his house.

Notice the relationship between our "belief—doubt—belief" model and what actually, observably happens to the Philippian jailer. He begins, first, with a well-fixed belief. He thoroughly believes that Paul and Silas belong in his jail. It is, to him, a piece of certain knowledge. If we review verses 16–24, we see why he thinks this is so.

16 And it came to pass as we went to prayer, a certain damsel possessed with a spirit of divination, met us, which brought her masters much gain by soothsaying: 17 The same followed Paul and us, and cried, saying, These men are the servants of the most high God, which shew unto us the way of salvation. 18 And this did she many days. But Paul being grieved, turned and said to the spirit, I command thee in the name of Jesus Christ to come out of her. And he came out the same hour. 19 And when her masters saw that the hope of their gains was gone, they caught Paul and Silas, and drew them into the market-place unto the rulers, 20 And brought them to the magistrates, saying, These men, being Jews, do exceedingly trouble our city, 21 And teach customs which are not lawful for us to receive, neither to observe, being Romans. 22 And the multitude rose up together against them: and the magistrates rent off their clothes, and commanded to beat them. 23 And when they had laid many stripes upon them, they cast them into prison, charging the jailer to keep them safely. 24 Who having received such a charge, thrust them into the inner prison, and made their feet fast in the stocks.

The jailer is certain that Paul and Silas belong in his jail because the magistrates ordered their arrests; the magistrates appear here as his superiors and as competent authorities in Roman law. They ordered these arrests because the "masters" of the fortune teller or soothsayer, seeing a destruction of their profits at hand, cited what they took to be a proscription in Roman law against practicing objectionable or disruptive customs as an argument for the imprisonment of Paul and Silas. But were these masters themselves competent authorities in Roman law, or just emotionally attached to their profits? Were the magistrates reasonable in making judgments based on such claims? And are not the members of the aroused mob also being ruled by their emotions, rather than by their potential to be clear-headed eyewitnesses? Emotions play a role, perhaps quite a large role, in our acquisition and development of knowledge; but surely we do not want questions such as these decided mainly by our emotions!

This specific chain of events contains at least two informal fallacies best avoided in argumentation generally, namely, accepting an illegitimate authority and accepting uninformed consensus as legitimate sources and kinds of evidence. In this case the "masters" and the crowd are the generative factors. These fallacies are known, respectively, as *argument from authority* and *appeal to the mob*.

But the jailer, having received his orders from the magistrates, did not postpone his actions because of such logical difficulties. He had received orders from his superiors, and as far as he was concerned the prisoners delivered into his hands had been duly convicted and were his responsibility to keep locked up. The jailer's duty and belief system were perfectly in tune, and after securing his prisoners he no doubt retired for an evening of untroubled sleep.

At this point, the jailer has surely accepted an argument from authority by the magistrates, who had been swayed by the masters' claim and by the appeal of the mob. He probably has also accepted two additional informal fallacies, namely, the masters' *ad hominem* attack on Paul and Silas as disruptive aliens and an *appeal to emotion* by the mob. An ad hominem argument appeals to prejudice by attacking a person's character rather than by mounting any objective evidence against that person's contentions. And an appeal to emotion is just that: an appeal to subjective emotion rather than an exhibition of actual evidence.

Now, let us take a closer look at the arrangement of the jailer's "reasons," and let us do so by way of being as explicit and clear as we can about the *formal* argument he has accepted. For he has indeed accepted, is following, and is prepared to act upon a formal argument of which he seems to be completely unaware.

The jailer has been confronted with a formal argument of the kind we describe as a *hypothetical* argument. You can think of a hypothetical argument as one in which at least one piece of evidence, one premise, is a *conditional* statement, namely, a statement that follows the "If . . .then . . ." pattern. Thus, one could easily construct the following argument of this sort: "It is my hypothesis, my guess, my prediction for the future, that *if* I fulfill the condition of seriously studying what I want to learn, *then* I will learn it well. I have seriously studied what I want to learn. Consequently, I have learned it well." In a nutshell, what this initial sort of hypothetical argument tries to do is to make explicit a linkage or relation between two sets of conditions or requirements, such that if the first or antecedent set appears, the second or consequent group should follow. Whether this relation is one producing absolute certainty or a kind of probability is not something we need to concern ourselves with at the moment. Nor do we need to concern ourselves at present with what relations there may be between a conditional statement's consequent and antecedent when considered *in that order*. It is this initial conditional relation of "If the antecedent conditions are present, then the consequent results will appear" that does interest our attention for now, especially when fleshed out in the illustration of the Philippian jailer.

Now, put yourself in the jailer's situation at just the moment when the order to imprison Paul and Silas had been uttered. The following hypothetical argument might pose itself.

Diagram 3.1

(*Premise no. 1*)

IF

(a) Paul and Silas have broken the law,

and

(b) the mob members, as witnesses, will attest to this,

and

(c) the magistrates thus judge them to be guilty,

and

(d) they order me to lock them up,

THEN

I must lock them up!

(*Premise no. 2*)

Conditions a, b, c, and d have indeed been fulfilled.

Thus, I must lock them up!

(*Conclusion*)

To this point, so far, so good for the jailer. All of the above seems like a reasonable enough procedure to him; convincing evidence is involved, he thinks, and he believes he will do well by himself to accept it. But the problem, of course, is that even in the midst of this formal argument, he has accepted as evidence items tainted by informal fallacies. In particular, the evidence of (b) above is weakened by the involvement of the mob and the emotions aroused. Likewise, the evidence of (c) is brought into question by the roles played by authority and *ad hominem* attacks.

In probable point of fact, given the jailer's past experience in such situations where Roman law seems to have been broken, where mob sentiment confirms this sort of observation, and where the relevant magistrate has pronounced guilt, the jailer would not have even pondered the merits of this specific case for very long. That is, all of these events, thus far, agree with his beliefs, his habits, his "already-knowns." But then came the first part of his initial problem, namely, the earthquake. Surely a bit of doubt arose in his mind as a result: "This does not fit into my experience with the world at all!" Then came the second part of his initial problem: "Now wait, how is it that all the cells are now unlocked and all the stocks undone? All my prisoners have escaped and have run away!" Now a real problem has arisen for him, a problem real enough that he is prepared to kill himself over it: "This is my knowledge of such things, and this was my duty—my knowledge, namely, that locking Paul and Silas up was right, I still hold to be true; but I have failed altogether in my duty—my prisoners are loose. For this I will be held responsible. Now, in spite of my best but hasty efforts to examine all of this in a rational light, my final duty is clear. Or at least my fear of being dealt with by those damned magistrates and that mob is clear enough!" The jailer and his "reasons" wriggle against these circumstances that contradict his past experience, but they cannot, it seems, escape what appears to be quite clear-cut and final. And so he draws his sword to commit suicide. But the resolution of his doubt, of course, was perhaps literally just around the corner.

There are three points to notice and ponder in this illustration as a whole. The first we have already dwelt on at some length, but it is now time to make this point as explicitly and clearly as we can. It is this: the Philippian jailer proceeded, right up to and including the moment of starting to kill himself, according to the best principles of rationality and experience available to him. His "belief—doubt—belief" system was solid and intact. It was *so* intact for him that actually taking his own life, as a means to escape his problem, made sense to him! All of this seemed completely rational to him.

This only goes to reinforce an observation made time and time again by Peirce, namely, that when we are confronted with a real, living, obstinate doubt, we will resort to almost *anything*, including self-deception, in attempting to resolve that doubt and progress or return to a condition of settled belief and habit. Now, while it is not being suggested that the jailer deluded himself about any of this business, in our example it remains quite clear that he was quite ready to attempt the ultimate "anything" to resolve his problem and the unbearable doubt it caused him.

The second point to bear in mind is that the resolution of his doubt, his release from this rational-seeming box from which death appears to him to be the only plausible escape, occurs in a nonrational manner. Now, yes, if you read a little further in the account you find that, as Paul and Silas were in fact Roman citizens and thus entitled to a formal hearing before being beaten and imprisoned, the whole bungled affair was from the beginning a legal mistake. The eventual resolution of the legal problem was, of course, a rational one. But what you should address your attention to is the immediate "moment of truth" for our jailer. At the moment *his* doubt is relieved, at his moment of religious experience, he uses no reasoning at all.

The jailer does not have his religious experience, his religious "moment of truth," based on a process of weighing the costs and benefits of rival religious groups in a rational, almost business-like manner. In reviewing verses 29–31 we see that when his moment arrives, the truth is, to him, undeniable *and unreasoned*. We might safely assume, perhaps, that after his moment of revelation or conversion, he proceeded with his life, yet again, in what to him seemed like a completely rational manner, especially given this new "premise" in his own belief system.

A third consideration from this exercise with hypothetical argument deals with the relations we see among rationality, irrationality, and nonrationality. For it seems, based on this evidence, that (a) rationally fixed belief can lead to irrational and disastrous consequences, (b) a true, living doubt generated in purely rational ways may, at times, be resolvable only by nonrational means, and (c) irrational effects and nonrational resolutions can produce rational tendencies. So, there do not appear, at least for now, to be any relations or connections among these three modes of belief that involve some sort of "guarantee" as far as the results or consequences of their use are concerned. That is, neither rational, nor irrational, nor nonrational fixations of belief seem to be accompanied by guarantees that ensure their stability once they have appeared. To attempt to force these modes of belief into fixed, inflexible, anti-pragmatic forms actually narrows our options among the various raw materials used for knowing anything. In other words, these three modes—belief, habit, and knowledge—cannot be open to every possible option for acquiring and developing our knowledge. Indeed, we should not try to handle these modes of belief according to some sort of dogmatic, mechanically executable recipe that supposedly will, before and even in defiance of experimentation, produce absolutely guaranteed and desirable results.

Had the jailer dogmatically or mechanically clung to his belief, to his "already-known" view of the world, it seems it would have cost him his life at his own hand. But, instead of being a dogmatist, he recognized the doubt-provoking events occurring all around him and entered into an experiment that promptly resulted in a resolution of his doubt. There is a general observation to be made here about the experience of the jailer that reveals two primary interlocking aspects of what we can take to be the basic or fundamental method of truly knowing anything: thoroughgoing, rote dogmatism thwarts the acquisition and development of human knowledge, while pragmatism or experimentalism promotes them both. Dogmatism did not work for the jailer, and it will not work for us.

An examination of our private emotional states and of our artistic apprehensions has considerable bearing on this point of view about the relationship among nonrational insight, rational and irrational conducts of life, and dogmatism. Consider, for a moment, the intriguing business we like to call falling in love. Analogous to the jailer's moment of conversion, our experiences of falling in love may indeed be preceded and followed by various rational or irrational efforts, but at the moment of the experience, no reasoning seems involved at all. And, just like the jailer's conversion, falling in love may seem, at the time, to solve a number of our problems. For example, from time to time many of us experience genuine and profound doubt about ourselves or about how we are getting on in the world. And we can become terribly dogmatic in this sort of doubt, even in spite of plenty of commonsense observations to the contrary. Falling in love can resolve this sort of doubt, at least for a while. But, then, so can getting drunk, at least for a while.

Yet whereas a nonrational insight resolved the jailer's doubt in a more savory manner than a maintenance of dogmatism would have, can the same be said for a profound transition in our private emotional states like falling in love? Indeed so. Just as the jailer's nonrational conversion literally saved his life, so the nonrational act of falling in love seems, at times, to prevent people from engaging in similarly self-destructive acts. And, of course, although falling in love with another person is doubtless the most familiar variety of this activity, it is not exclusive in this respect. We all know persons who appear to be quite in love with things other than other persons: the amateur sailor with his sailboat, the home craftsman with his workshop, the fanatically loyal fan with his football team. At any rate, by way of continuing our examination of nonrational resolution of doubt and fixation of belief, let us examine an illustration concerned with love and reason that balances both aesthetically and logically with the experience of the jailer's conversion.

One of the most disturbing kinds of irrational behavior, of clinging dogmatically to an already-known system of belief, involves the crime known, curiously enough, as "domestic violence." The problem is disturbing both because this category of criminal behavior usually involves men (husbands more often than not) beating up women and because this activity is far more pervasive in our society than official statistics might suggest. Let us suppose a hypothetical case of domestic violence and examine the reasoning of the victim. Such a case would surely involve, for any ordinary sane person, a condition of doubt as strong as any to be ordinarily encountered. The relevant, intensely private questions must arise, I would think, according to some schema like: "I married this person because of love, and yet now I am being physically abused, and regularly, by this same person who supposedly loves me. Does this person really love me, or not? Do I, any longer, really love this person, or not?" This person is trapped, probably in more than just one way. But our question should address how this fundamental variety of doubt, this knowledge-issue, might be handled. And while they must never be completely ignored in such cases, please try to put the physical, financial, geographical, and other probably enormous material considerations of the victim aside for the moment and ask what, in terms of human knowledge and our methods for acquiring and developing it, could occur in such a situation to resolve this doubt?

Now in principle, it seems that the victim here is in exactly the same situation as the jailer was formerly. That is, a comfortable, probably doubt-free condition is put in jeopardy by external, autonomous circumstances. A dogmatic clinging to the "already known" will but perpetuate the doubt and the misery that accompanies it. An experimental resolution of the doubt that this dogmatism reinforces is possible, but it seems to be possible only in a nonrational way. The victim's friends and relatives, just like an easily imagined group of the jailer's cronies, can express their sympathy all they wish, and they might even try rational persuasion to assuage the relevant doubt, but until this present victim has his or her moment of *nonrational* insight and *sees* that there is no love left in this relationship, dogmatism and doubt will prevail.

Again, dogmatism thwarts the acquisition and development of human knowledge, while experimentalism promotes them both. Dogmatism will either (a) drive the victim back into the same situation of doubt, or, as some suggest, (b) simply replicate this doubt in a subsequent situation. And further as with the case of the jailer, an experimental, nonrational resolution of doubt here carries with it, in and of itself, no guarantee whatsoever that it will remain stable or lead to any "preset" results in either rational or irrational areas. But we know that dogmatism did not work for the jailer, and now we know that it will not work for the victim. Can it work for us in any other context?

A third area in which nonrational insight seems predominant, and where dogmatism has yet another sort of role to play, is the area of artistic expression and appreciation. The immediate or "brute force" nature of our apprehensions in the arts seems quite like the experiences of religious conversion and falling in love that we have already examined. That is, one may reason all one likes before and after a moment of profound artistic experience, but at the actual moment of the experience, no reasoning seems involved at all. In fact, it seems that an excessive amount of reasoning of a certain sort in these matters may yield only a staunch form of dogmatism. Consider, then, one general example from the visual arts and some very general remarks on classical music.

Most of us who do not spend much time looking into all the intricacies of art history have a sort of "realistic" expectation of the visual arts. That is, we generally expect paintings, for instance, to look like that which they represent. As an example, take a moment to examine the French impressionist Auguste Renoir's *Monet Working in His Garden,* painted in 1873 (see Gaunt 1970: 96). It does not take any great power of reasoning to detect something relaxing and calming, if you will, in this work. Everything in it seems familiar enough to us. We easily recognize the houses in the background, the trees, flowers, and wooden fence in the middle distance, and the figure of Monet with painting equipment in use that occupies the foreground. All these various parts seem to unite, effortlessly, into a coherent whole. It seems, as a whole, to "click" nonrationally into place for us. Nothing startles us in this work, nothing taxes our powers of reasoning; everything in it "looks" just as it should. In fact, the flowers seem so real, even in their two-dimensional plane, that we are tempted to reach out and try to pick one.

By contrast, spend a few minutes with the early fifteenth-century work by Hubert and/or Jan Van Eyck entitled *The Last Judgment* (see Janson 1966: 275). What do we see here? At the very least, what we see is not a depiction of a reality that is as familiar to us as was Renoir's. Is it actually a depiction of reality at all? We see what appears to be a graduated continuum of beings ranging from Christ and several angels at the top of the frame down to, at the bottom, a half-dozen or so satanic-looking beasts surrounded by a chaotic mob of souls of the damned. Now this is not a reality, if it is a reality at all, that is easily familiar to us. It looks "wrong" to us overall. And there are some identifiable details that contribute directly to our puzzlement. Consider for a moment just the area of the work that deals with the region above hell. To our eyes, there are at least three major problems with this presentation. First, we note that all the beings depicted, except those falling into hell, are suspended in the sky. This violates our commonsense expectations about gravity. Second, the figures of Christ, Mary, and Joseph are markedly larger than the saints, clerics, and people of means immediately beneath them, who in turn are markedly larger than the condemned. This does not agree with our general observation that people do not vary in size, as they do here, by a factor of four. Third, something does not seem quite right with the attempt at perspective. The gigantic size of Christ, relatively speaking, seems somehow to nullify or at least make uncertain the attempt at a three-dimensional effect. What could be the meaning of all of this?

Obviously, this work is not realistic to our modern, Western minds. This work does not, and will not, "click" into place for us so long as we dogmatically cling to the same expectations as were so easily satisfied by *Monet Working in His Garden*. That is, the unruffled belief with which we approached and departed Renoir's work has now been challenged; doubt has arisen. And just as with the jailer and the victim of domestic violence, if we cling tenaciously to our "already knowns" in this circumstance this doubt will remain unresolved. What is it that we must come to know in this example that will lead to a new, secure fixation of belief? What we must come to know is a reality strikingly different from the one familiar to the modern, Western mind, namely, the reality of the medieval mind, the reality of the Middle Ages.

Now the dogmatist, in an attempt to rescue his or her belief, would maintain that *The Last Judgment* was put together by an incompetent. "After all," the dogmatist would say, "everybody knows that people cannot suspend themselves in mid-air, that they do not vary so wildly in size, and that we live in a clearly three-dimensional world precisely describable by physics." But this, of course, is exactly the point. *The Last Judgment*, as a product of the Medieval mind, is not concerned with any sort of accuracy with regard to physical size, the very sort of unfounded accuracy that has our dogmatist in a rant, but rather is pre-occupied with a sort of accuracy with regard to theological size. That this is not an accident confined to the Van Eyck work is attested to by the fact that in 1420, about the time *The Last Judgment* was painted, only about one painting out of every twenty was on a subject other than religion (see Burke 1985: 78). And the rendering of religious subject matter in this work is not accidental, either. Nor is it the work of an incompetent. To the medieval mind it was only *natural* to have the theologically important figures suspended in the sky because, after all, that was the direction in which heaven was to be found. Likewise, Christ, Mary, and Joseph should be four times larger than the poor souls slipping into hell because they are, theologically considered, at least four times more important. And of course the looming figure of Christ can muddle up the seeming attempt at a three-dimensional perspective because Christ, as a part of the Holy Trinity, need pay no heed to ordinary rules of physical reality at all. All these, and similar considerations, made for something which, to the medieval mind, made sense.

Perhaps the most important thing to observe in this example is that *The Last Judgment* was not, for the medieval mind, only an exercise in preparing a canvas or a brush technique or the production of colored paints or other matters of technical interest. For medieval minds, this work depicted the way reality actually was, and it was that way for them, as a belief, just as strongly and securely as our belief that Newtonian and quantum physics accurately depicts our modern, everyday reality. This painting, then, in its context, was a "written down" version of the best explanatory hypothesis that medieval investigators had for how the universe actually worked. And we can rationally, and ruthlessly, consider the various aspects of comparative theological size, suspensions of the law of gravity, mismanagements of perspective, salvation, damnation, and what not, and still "miss the point": for medieval minds this *was* reality, and it was a reality that was unyielding. As a work of art and as a description of reality, we cannot fully absorb "the point" here, if indeed the modern mind can absorb it in more than a superficial way at all, in any other than a nonrational and experimental manner. Can we really see this work as a profound expression of another reality by simply, rationally, and mechanically, reciting to ourselves a list of all the details that contribute to it? Assuredly not. Now, of course, we can make such rational ponderings before and after we have had our moment of insight into this other world, but it does not appear that we can have that very insight except in a nonrational way. And an experimental, trial-and-error method for reaching such a nonrational insight seems to be the method we most often employ toward this end.

A few comments on the subject of classical music generally and piano music in particular may shed more light. This latter subject is one I have been familiar with for a long time. Speaking from singular, personal experience in such matters is of course highly risky if generalizable principles are sought, but perhaps one or two personal observations will not hinder our inquiry. I can clearly recall a handful of occasions when, as a concert player, all the aspects involved in a performance "clicked" into place. All the preparations, hundreds of hours of practicing, rehearsals, deciphering of musical scores, and so forth, seemed to have been but an enormous rational, but mostly "hidden," prologue to a sustained moment of nonrational, artistic enlightenment. My belief that these occasions were not merely moments of subjective self-delusion or indulgence was bolstered by the fact that audiences seemed likewise to have been "inspired." Audiences know, after all, when a performer is insincere, when there seems to be a contradiction between what the performer is actually doing and what he or she is presumably attempting; and they know this, at least in part, at a nonrational level.

The best general description I have been able to muster for these moments and occasions when everything seemed to fall into place is that they form an imprecise combination of the religious, the emotional, and the artistic. More precisely and prosaically, these moments seem similar to descriptions offered by athletes of particularly successful efforts in sports activities. In the cases of both the artist and the athlete, three phenomena are often associated with profound experiences: (1) a seeming suspension of the orderly passage of time, (2) a kind of effortless precision in execution, and (3) fierce but somehow relaxed mental concentration that produces an almost objective detachment from the activity itself. One seems, at one and the same time, to be a deeply involved participant and yet also a detached, almost neutral, observer. No reasoning whatsoever seems involved at such moments, and no recipe or mechanically executed routine will produce this end. The subject of music is, thus, an elusive one to examine for these purposes.

So it seems indeed to be the case in some religious, emotional, and artistic matters that nonrational insight, gained through a kind of experimentation rather than attempted through a kind of rote, mechanistic routine, has a redoubtable role to play in our acquisition and development of knowledge. But there are, of course, limits to the scope of nonrational insight. We would find it quite unsettling, for instance, should a judge and jury pronounce a verdict, a medical organization decide about an organ transplant, the Internal Revenue Service ponder a lien on our property, or a university professor record a semester's grade based solely on a supposed nonrational insight. No one would or should, for example, accept a failing grade in a course when the professor in charge claims the following as the rationale: "Well, I had a really intense nonrational insight into all of this business about your grade for the term, and so I have decided that you are going to get an F in this course because (a) God spoke to me and told me that this is the grade you should receive, or (b) emotionally I detest you, so I will psychologically erode you with this grade, or (c) your physical presence is aesthetically repulsive to me, so I will drive you away with this grade. The grades you may have actually earned during this course are completely irrelevant in the matter."

This would be a most unsatisfactory state of affairs because the decision here has been a *subjective* one rather than an *objective* one. What is the difference? Roughly put, a conclusion based on subjective considerations is usually little more than a matter of purely personal opinion, while a conclusion based on objective considerations is one drawn in comparison to matters that are, to some degree at least, *independent* of personal opinion. The affair concerning the grade is of course a subjective matter, one that asserts a contradiction between recorded performance and the final grade that supposedly reflects such performance. In contrast, the conclusion that water, under certain identifiable and repeatable conditions, boils at 212 degrees Fahrenheit is based on the occurrence of a phenomenon whose occurrence itself is completely independent of what we may think of it. As indispensable as creative, experimental exercises of nonrational insight are for the acquisition and development of our knowledge, however, they themselves, being at the moment of their very occurrence independent of our reasoning processes, cannot be rationally justified in that moment. That is, how could we nonrationally challenge our professor friend in such as way as to demonstrate, objectively and unequivocally, that his supposedly nonrational religious, emotional, and aesthetical insights were just plain wrong?

The problem, of course, is that we cannot construct such a *challenge*, precisely considered, on solely nonrational grounds, and we are prevented from doing so because, given the nature of nonrational insight, the best we can hope for is but a different expression of subjectivism, a contradictory expression of the same fundamental problem. In principle, this sort of seemingly irresolvable conflict must have been on the mind of the pianist Artur Schnabel (1882–1951) when he commented that "the classification of right or wrong [has no] validity for music, which is beyond being measured and judged by quantity or by 'moral' standards" (Schnabel 1942: 16). A nonrational insight in and of itself is not capable of rational criticism. But its practical effects, both observable and conceivable, *are* subject and must be subjected to rational criticism if a claim to knowledge is made, and particularly when we wish to take care that our nonrational insights do not become irrational. The nonrational insight when subjected to criticism may become knowledge. Thus, again applying Schnabel's comments about music analogically to the issue of nonrationalism overall, we find that our nonrational insight and subsequent developments of human knowledge may yet move us "toward that other shore which, to be sure, can only be sighted but never reached" (Schnabel 1942: 14). I will argue in the final chapter that nonrational insight must be sustained by pragmatic criticism if irrational consequences are to be avoided. It is important, then, that we become familiar with some basic principles of reasoning that contribute to pragmatic, rational criticism and fixations of belief. Such principles are focused in studies of logic.

4

Logic and Creativity

■ *Logic comes in two varieties: one sort is narrow and technical, a discipline many find a little frightening; the other is broader and more ingrained in our daily lives, the sort represented by our pragmatic logic of events. Our pragmatic logic itself, however, often depends on the narrower variety, and creativity and criticism are required to use either type of logic properly. In distinguishing the essential differences between these two forms of logic, we find that the Peirce-Marquand logic machine, an early form of the modern computer, can actually perform the operations of a portion of the narrower logic.*

*W*HEN THE ordinary person hears the term "logic," the response is often a mixture of fear and confusion. Logic in the older, broader sense, the overall pragmatic logic of events described in chapter 1, is not ordinarily the object of this fear. Fear of logic generally comes from exposure to one of the narrower and more technical forms of syllogistic, propositional, or quantificational logic. We shall have occasion to find some items from syllogistic and propositional logic useful for the deductive phase of our logic of events. But because fear is only likely to get in the way of our investigation, let us look further into this issue of fear and logic.

Many people have the vague notion that logic has something to do with mathematics, or at least that it *looks* like something mathematical, and because so many people are afraid of mathematics, mentioning "logic" triggers fear. Of course, this association of logic with mathematics, and of mathematics with fear—thus producing an association of logic with fear—is itself *an instance of logical inference*. But even if such fear is abated, the association of logic and mathematics is firm in many people's minds. Look at the following examples from the field of propositional logic and notice how the precise arrangement of symbols and notations suggests similarities with certain forms of mathematics.

Diagram 4.1

$$p :: (p \lor p)$$
$$p :: (p \cdot p)$$
$$(p \lor q) :: (q \lor p)$$
$$(p \cdot q) :: (q \cdot p)$$
$$[p \lor (q \lor r)] :: [(p \lor q) \lor r]$$
$$[p \cdot (q \cdot r)] :: [(p \cdot q) \cdot r]$$
$$[p \cdot (q \lor r)] :: [(p \cdot q) \lor (p \cdot r)]$$
$$[p \lor (q \cdot r)] :: [(p \lor q) \cdot (p \lor r)]$$

(see Hurley 1997: 402; 392)

We will also see that logic is commonly and reasonably associated in people's minds with computers. In fact, we shall investigate an interesting connection between logic and computers a little later.

Those people who have a "deer in the headlights" response to logic usually have the mistaken notion that it is something horribly complicated, dry, and dull in the extreme, riddled with hair-splitting intellectual traps, and therefore either a tiresome drudgery or something to be feared. Because of those vague associations between logic on the one hand and mathematics and computers on the other, those people may think that to become fluent in logic they must learn to think and behave rather like machines, which is not an attractive prospect for most. When they juxtapose what they initially think logic may require against their generally non-mechanistic images of themselves, people simply feel conflicted and uncomfortable.

This sort of internal conflict can be thought of as a pairing or conjunction of contradicting observations or beliefs, one claiming that something *is* the case at a given moment and in some particular aspect, the other, at the very same time and in the very same aspect, claiming that something *is not* the case. For example, the pairing "this electrical switch is now on" and "this electrical switch is now off" represents, given that "now" refers to the same moment in time, a contradiction; the two are contradictory statements. Likewise, the pairing "people *are* really machines, at root" and "people *are not* really so, at root" represents a contradiction. The so-called law of non-contradiction, as a basic ingredient of our thought and understanding, forbids this sort of pairing of contradictory notions. So, if we use 'P' to indicate 'people', the sign '~' to represent 'not', and the sign '·' to represent conjunction or 'and', our dilemma, and the law of non-contradiction, can be tidily summarized as follows: we cannot have 'P · ~P' ('P' and not 'P').

Thus, from our present case arises a seemingly irresolvable friction of a definite sort between two strongly held beliefs, these beliefs being represented by 'P' and '~P'. For how could it be, we ask, that we as human beings are just logical or calculating *machines*? How can the creative part of us—the part that makes guesses and mistakes, the part that uses a "trial and error," experimental, pragmatic approach to solve problems, the part of us that seems to learn, to expand our knowledge, and to allow life to be enjoyable—how can that part of us remain alive if we are defined as and required to behave like such machines? For many of us, this is a serious question that expresses a fundamental doubt about our status in our current era: surely human behavior cannot be utterly standardized and so potentially mechanized, because people are not machines. Yet we can, in *principle* at least, logically resolve this doubt and attendant contradiction.

We have already applied the conjunctive law of non-contradiction, as one side of a coin, to our predicament. We can now employ its disjunctive twin, the so-called "law of excluded middle," from the other side of the same coin to allow us to choose between contradictory options. If we again use 'P' to indicate 'people' and '~' to indicate 'not', but now use 'v' to indicate the disjunctive relation 'or', or better yet, '*either* ___ or ___' we arrive at, not a contradiction, but the disjunction 'P v ~P' (either 'P' or not 'P'). So, logically at least, the intolerable contradiction with its opposed components now becomes, for us, the welcomed disjunction within which a choice between those opposed components can be made. But how can we actually *apply* this seemingly sterile piece of reasoning to our problem of people and machines? Again, in *principle* at least, a relatively easy solution is at hand if we can answer the question, Are human beings really different from machines, be they mathematical machines, logical machines, or otherwise? We can answer this question affirmatively because our creative capacities clearly exceed the limits of machine computability, the limits of following a type of recipe that all computing machines must follow. Put another way, our abilities exceed the limits of following the "fixed method" diagnosed by Peirce in "Our Senses as Reasoning Machines" (1900), quoted in chapter 3.

Obviously, we are different from machines in our pragmatic, experimental ability to be creative. When it comes to mathematics or logic or geology or literature or any other learnable subject matter, achieving a real understanding that persists over time and can be trusted, tested experimentally, and then discarded or retained or improved upon, we really do have to employ all the creativity we can muster. The genuine acquisition and development of human knowledge, therefore, hinges on a critical creativity that allows for that trust and use, encourages testing, permits rejection or maintenance, and delights in conceivable improvement of our knowledge. This long-term creative process is known as experimentalism or pragmatism.

We must make this acquisition and development of knowledge "our own," so to speak. Simple mechanical repetitions or rote memorization of "facts" in the name of satisfying an immediate but transitory demand, like passing an academic or training examination, usually have a predictable outcome. We memorize what is required for some immediate purpose, and as soon as that purpose has passed we more or less thoroughly forget it all. But a different outcome is also possible. If we detect in our array of facts a stable logic or developmental pattern, our memory can actively and creatively secure the information more durably. A computing machine can usefully perform the rather mindless operations involved in the first outcome, and it can perform these operations faster and more reliably than any of us can or ever will. But only a creative, pragmatic intelligence can expect to enjoy the profits available from, but never guaranteed by, the second outcome and the experimental process associated with it.

This brings us to an often-overlooked yet important point about creativity, experimental method, and pragmatism. A certain minimal, indispensable amount of what we sometimes call rote memorization may be necessary at the outset in order to proceed effectively in acquiring and developing genuine knowledge. This is particularly true when we enter some department of knowledge that is completely new to us. Embarking on such a study may require us to memorize some new and fundamental tools, like a specialized vocabulary or an unfamiliar system of abstract notation or some other set of facts and relations, just in the name of "getting started." After the novelty of a new field or task has passed and the new knowledge associated with it can be handled with facility or even habitually, our tentative beginning efforts are often forgotten. By then, we see *why* certain facts and relations behave as they do and not just *how* they so behave. Yet we still retain the basic tools or raw materials that we initially needed to begin our experimental journey toward this region of facility, and we retain these tools by a far more secure procedure than rote memorization. Even though we may sometimes forget information that we think we have carefully stored, we can, in fact, bring it back into play and act upon it. Everyone knows the value of clinging to some facts through rote memorization just long enough to parrot them back for an examination. But it is only through application of those facts and results, through accounting for *why* and not just *how*, that we find a genuine development of knowledge. The often misunderstood phenomenon of biological evolution, about which we shall have more to say later, is an old, yet living and breathing example of this sort of genuine, pragmatic knowledge. Conversely, a mechanical, uncreative and *dogmatic* adoption of any particular "knowledge creed," including misunderstood varieties of pragmatism itself, only blocks the road of inquiry.

An analog in the field of music may help to illustrate at least part of the meaning here. There is a black key roughly in the middle of the keyboard on an ordinary piano, forty-three keys from the bottom of the keyboard and forty-six keys from the top, known as an "E flat." There are six other keys on an ordinary piano keyboard also known as "E flat," but our focus is on the one in the middle. Ordinary musical notation assigns a written mark or sign that corresponds to each and every key on an ordinary piano keyboard. So this one key or note that we call "E flat" has its own, individual, notational sign.

And this particular notation, this mark or sign, corresponds *exactly* to that one note on the piano keyboard and to no other. Each of the other six E flats has its specific and characteristic notation as well. In the nineteenth century the Hungarian-born pianist and composer Franz Liszt composed two piano concertos, the first of which is in the key of E-flat major. Without going into a complicated explanation of what "key" means in this more general sense, it is sufficient for our purposes here to say that this concerto, this work for piano soloist and orchestra, is absolutely loaded with hundreds of E-flats. Here is the point: if one does not somehow already know, through memorization and recall, that these various spots on the musical score correspond exactly and without any exception whatsoever to certain keys on the keyboard, one cannot even begin to learn, much less understand and perform, this concerto. Once the musical and not just the optical association between notation and piano key has been sufficiently established as habit or unconscious response, this mechanical sort of recall can be dispensed with. But in the beginning, for most people, some amount of rote, mechanistic memorization is required for learning to play the piano. Surely our first exposure to any new and strange vocabulary or system of abstract notation must include room for that initial stage of simple memorization and recall. Otherwise, how can we begin?

However that may be, when we genuinely acquire and develop knowledge, we are traveling across a broad continuum or spectrum of types of learning, ranging all the way from the largely rote and mechanical, perhaps in getting started, to the predominantly creative, experimental, and pragmatic. Advancement along this spectrum or continuum will indeed involve making some "mistakes" that can be pragmatically "corrected" along the way. But one's overall evolution of knowledge must be allowed to move through this continuum, without either stagnation or abrupt interruption. That is, to dwell exclusively on the mechanistic end of this spectrum must yield a kind of mental stagnation, and to move abruptly to the "creative" or "experimental" end of the spectrum, without solid grounding in the fundamentals, denies the objective demands of a creative or experimental method and can only produce the vacuous and inane.

But what has all this to do with logic, with right reasoning, with being as rational as we can in our fixations of belief? If we employ our logical principles, our principles of rationality, only in that purely mechanistic, rote fashion such as the computing machine is pre-eminently capable of, then ironically we risk an outcome for ourselves that is irrational and unproductive. Again, if we do not actually act upon and consciously use a pragmatic, experimental method in our reasoning processes, then we are no better off than the machine, and just as capable of being led astray, of being mastered and manufactured. Some further remarks from Peirce's "Our Senses as Reasoning Machines" (1900), quoted in chapter 3, bear repetition here.

. . . so we do when we go irreflectively by a rule of thumb, as when we apply a rule of arithmetic [or logic] the reason of which we have never been taught [or genuinely learned]. The irrationality here consists in our following a fixed method, of the correctness of which the other method [experimentalism or pragmatism] affords no assurance; so that if it [the fixed method] does not happen to be right in its application to the case at hand, we go hopelessly astray. In genuine reasoning, we are not wedded to our method. We deliberately approve it, but we stand ever ready and disposed to reexamine it and to improve upon it, and to criticize our criticism of it, without cessation (Peirce 1900, MS 831: 11).

So logic, if we are truly to make it "our own," so to speak, cannot be merely a dry husk that we mechanically pull out of our "reasoning drawer" and invoke every now and then to brush the intellectual dust off our beliefs. To quote Peirce again on the joint subject of logic and reasoning, "It is a *LIVING* process" (Peirce 1887b, my emphasis). And it is a living process that finds its way into every university classroom, onto every factory floor and, whether we clearly perceive and acknowledge it or not, into every facet of our lives.

Logic, as we have defined it, is the study of arguments, and our focus is on the larger sort we know as our pragmatic logic of events. The two large categories *within* pragmatic logical argument that we will be concerned with are the deductive area and the inductive area. Deductive logic, when applied properly, produces conclusions from the evidence supplied that are matters of certainty. Given our fallibility, we here knowingly and consciously work with *practical* certainty, but always with the possibility and aim in mind of correction of our errors against *ideal* certainty. Inductive logic, when properly applied, produces from obtained evidence conclusions that are matters of probability and, in the course of things, degrees of probability. Again, given our fallible natures, inductive logic also has both practical and ideal aspects.

We shall now examine five illustrations of deductive arguments and one broad example of inductive argumentation. Here are our five illustrative categories of deductive arguments:

(1) categorical syllogism using one combination of universal, affirmative propositions;
(2) disjunctive syllogism in two distinct versions;
(3) pure hypothetical syllogism;
(4) arguments of the form *modus ponens;*
(5) arguments of the form *modus tollens.*

Our first illustration, as its name implies, is drawn from the rather large subject of categorical syllogistic logic, while our four other illustrations are taken from propositional logic. We will spend more time on categorical syllogism than on the others. But its deductive implications are not peculiar to it; they also hold for its four propositional companions.

Actually, there are 256 different varieties of categorical syllogisms, but we shall be concerned here only with the following example. You should read and understand the three propositions composing it in a straightforward, literal way. Take care to notice that the three collections of things or sets or classes involved—namely "human beings," "mammals," and things that are "warm-blooded"—are of three different population sizes. Recalling our discussion of *argument* in chapter 3, the evidence section of an argument is given in a 'premise' or in 'premises'. Thus:

Syllogism 1

All human beings are mammals.
All mammals are warm-blooded.

Therefore, all human beings are warm-blooded.

The first sentence is the first premise, the second sentence is the second premise, and the final sentence, as "Therefore" implies, is the conclusion. Notice also that there are three terms at issue in the argument: "human beings," "mammals" and "warm-blooded." All categorical syllogisms are arguments reaching a conclusion through the use of two premises constructed of three terms. Readers already familiar with standard-form syllogistic logic may object that this example mixes 'mood' and 'figure' in a non-standard manner by reversing the traditional ordering of the two premises. This departure, however, provides us with a more quickly and thoroughly understood illustration of the inevitability of deductive reasoning and its necessary character (see Hurley 1994: 52). (This departure works especially well when working with Euler diagrams, as are used later, at diagram 4.3, to illustrate a *four*-term categorical deductive argument.)

The example given above is called a categorical syllogism because each of its components addresses a category or class of things: "all human beings," "all mammals," and, by implication, "all things that are warm-blooded." We see that the conclusion is supported by our two premises, and we see that the connection between premises and conclusion, the reasoning involved, ensures this support. That is, we see certain *relations* between the classes of things themselves, and we see that these relations bring us inevitably to the conclusion. When we use categorical reasoning, as we do here, we thus work with the logical relations of classes. In this case, the variety of reasoning is deductive because from two pieces of evidence it has produced a conclusion that is a matter of certainty. Some find this notion that evidence only "supports" a conclusion to be a bit elastic for deductive purposes; something a bit stronger seems needed. The relation between evidence and conclusion in a properly done deductive argument, then, might be tightened, more like a relation of cause and effect, even when the term "supports" is retained.

With regard to this issue of supporting evidence, and in contrast to the syllogism above, consider this example:

Syllogism 2

All human beings are mammals.
All warm-blooded creatures are mammals.

Therefore, all human beings are warm-blooded.

A true conclusion is offered, premises are presented that allegedly support it, some sort of an attempt at deductive reasoning seems to be in use, but something is not quite right here. The second premise, in particular, does not seem to be true. Are there not more members of the class or group called "warm-blooded" than just the members of the class or group known as "mammals," like birds? What is wrong with this illustration? How can it be that we seem to arrive at a conclusion that is true, but arrive by apparently faulty means? What is the value of such a conclusion, if it has any value at all?

This illustration is faulty in two aspects, and these two aspects must be properly handled if certainty in the conclusion of a deductive argument is our goal. These aspects are, first, the formal arrangement or pattern of the argument's parts and, second, the truth of the argument's premises. If we have a correct pattern of deductive argumentation we say that the argument form is *valid*. A valid argument form is such that it is impossible, given true premises, for the conclusion to be false. All five of the deductive argument types we are investigating have their valid forms. The first of our two syllogisms, above, has such a form. Ideally, a valid argument form that uses true premises exclusively will *necessarily* produce a true conclusion. That is, ideally, a deductive argument that so uses validity and truth together is said to be a *sound* argument. In all genuinely sound arguments, conclusions are matters of invariable truth and certainty: their truth matters not in the least on what we personally, or as groups, think of them. Thus, the conclusions of sound deductive arguments are matters of objective knowledge rather than matters of subjective opinion. Peirce put it succinctly when writing about such arguments: ". . .that from true premises they must invariably produce true conclusions" (*CP* 2.267). To deny the conclusion of a sound argument, then, asserts that the necessarily true conclusion is objectively inconsistent and in fact in contradiction with the argument's true premises.

If you think of "pattern" in much the same way that one might think of the master blueprints for a standardized series of buildings, the template used to guide the cutting of fabric toward assembling a garment, or a computer program, you will notice that there is a clear pattern to how the parts of syllogism 1 fit together. The first term of the first premise, "human beings," returns as the first term of the conclusion; the last term of the second premise, "warm-blooded," returns as the last term of the conclusion; and the term that seems to stand in the middle, "mammals," is represented twice in the premise materials in a kind of "diagonal" relation, but is not represented in the conclusion at all. With these items in mind, the internal pattern of terms used in the valid argument form of syllogism 1 may be summarized as follows.

Diagram 4.2

All *H*'s are *M*'s.
All *M*'s are *W*'s.

Therefore, all *H*'s are *W*'s.

Now we can clearly diagnose one of the two problems with syllogism 2: it has an *in*valid form. The five deductive arguments we are examining are all susceptible to having any number of invalid forms. Notice that the ordering of terms in the second premise of syllogism 2 is the reverse of what would allow for validity. This alone would render this argument unsound. But, further, we can also diagnose a second problem with this argument: the second premise is false. But do not conclude from this one example that making a premise false automatically nullifies its argument's validity. This too, alone, would produce an unsound argument. This premise is false because, as we noted above, there are indeed more members of the class "warm-blooded" than of the class "mammals." So, the argument of syllogism 1 is sound owing to its employment of a valid argument form and all true premises; the argument of syllogism 2 is *un*sound owing to its invalidity and also its use of a false premise. Once the possibility of a conclusion's guarantee of truth has been removed by invalidity or falsehood, a true conclusion that may nevertheless appear is, in a way, *accidentally* true. That is, its conclusion is not accompanied by any guarantee of truth, even though it does turn out to be true, as a matter of ordinary fact. And, furthermore, it bears repeating that either invalidity or a false premise will render an argument unsound. Only validity and true evidence, together, will yield certainty in the truth of their conclusion.

But how are truth and validity determined? Does truth have a role to play in determining validity? Of course, determining truth can also be a difficult business as well. The truth of such statements as "Stewart is alive" or "I am reading from Stewart's book" seems easy enough to determine for the moment. But what about statements like "God exists" or "Abortion, under any circumstance whatsoever, is a murderous, and therefore criminal, act"? Or, even more difficult, consider this contradicting pairing of statements:

"Everything I say, including the sentence that follows, is true."
"What I just said, above, is false."

Therefore, is my statment true when I say, "It is indeed true that 'Everything I say is true' is in fact false"? Or is it false? Obviously, *something* is wrong here.

In fact, it is easy to construct a completely valid argument form, as in the following syllogism 3, that nevertheless uses false premises. Here the terms used occur, diagrammatically, in our familiar valid pattern.

Syllogism 3

All lizards are mammals.
All mammals are geniuses.

Therefore, all lizards are geniuses.

So what, precisely, is the relation between truth and validity?

As the examples above illustrate, an argument's *validity* is a function of its internal structure, and the integrity of this structure itself cannot be inferred by the *actual* truth or falsity of the materials we employ in it. Deductive arguments composed of nonsense can still be formally valid, although we would need to make assumptions about truth to test such an argument's validity. In fact, making assumptions about truth to determine validity is standard procedure: we assume our premises true and then see if our conclusion follows with "strict necessity" (see Hurley 1997: 42). Likewise, if we assume the premises to be true and we know that the argument is valid, we must acknowledge the truth of the conclusion. And if we can justify our assumption that the premises are actually true, the resulting sound argument will compel our confidence in the truth of the conclusion. Validity itself, therefore, is not dictated by actual truth. It is this independence of validity from truth that makes possible the model of deductive logic for computer programming: computer programs and deductive arguments process or manipulate information supplied *to* them; but completely unflawed computer programs and standard forms of valid deductive arguments function with equal precision whether the information they manipulate is true or not. Likewise, the *invalidity* of deductive argument forms is completely independent of the actual combinations of truth and falsity of premises and conclusions—with one crucial exception: a deductive argument that uses all true premises and a false conclusion is, of necessity, an instance of an invalid argument form, for how else could a false conclusion occur in a deductive argument with all true premises? That is, no such valid argument from *exists,* even as an assumption. Consequently, if, on assuming the truth of our premises, we find that our conclusion is false, our argument is *proved invalid.*

But truth and falsity of argument materials otherwise can and do result in *either* valid or invalid forms. The certainty that we expect and that to an extent limits us in deduction would be clearly contradicted should we be able to assemble a supposedly valid deductive argument with true premises that nevertheless produced a false conclusion. What would your world be like if the computers that produce your paycheck, figure your bank statement, record the grades for your transcript, or verify your driver's license used a "logical" procedure capable of producing false conclusions from true and validly organized information? Your world would be reduced to chaos. We see then that the matching of true premises with a false conclusion in the real world necessarily can produce *only* an invalid and therefore unsound argument, and that the question of actual truth or falsity of argument materials is otherwise irrelevant to questions of validity and invalidity.

The necessary nature of deductive reasoning and its critical results in the pragmatic logic of events are indispensable instruments in our acquisition and development of knowledge. Their importance cannot be overemphasized. To illustrate further the matter of logical, objective necessity, let us take another look at the subjects of 'class' and 'relation' and add to them one further item, namely, the important notion of 'algorithm'.

Using citations from the definitions of 'class' and 'relation' supplied by Peirce in Whitney's *Century Dictionary*, we can understand better the subject of the logical relations of classes. For 'class' Peirce gave the following definition:

A number of objects distinguished by common characters from all others, and regarded as a collective unit or group; a collection capable of a general definition; a kind. (Peirce 1889: 1029)

For the following four-term illustration, then, let us count pianists, keyboard players, musicians, and artists as examples of different classes. The class or set of pianists, then, would be the class or set including and limited to all pianists.

For the term 'relation' Pierce gives the following definition:

A character of a plurality of things; a fact concerning two or more things, especially and more properly when it is regarded as a predicate of one of the things connecting it with the others; the condition of being such and such with regard to something else. (Peirce 1889: 5057)

Thus could we assert the relation of the classes "pianists" and "keyboardists" as "All pianists are keyboardists" and take it as the first premise of a *four*-term deductive argument. Because syllogisms are by definition limited to three terms and two premises, a deductive argument such as we are constructing, namely, one with *four* terms and *three* premises is not, strictly speaking, a syllogism, even though the principle of inference is the same.

Taking the first letters of these class names as abbreviations, we can state our first premise more briefly, in the following form. Thus, where 'P' abbreviates "pianists" and 'K' abbreviates "keyboardists," the proposition "All P is K" abbreviates this first premise. For greater clarity, we can also render this premise again in a modification of an Euler diagram or graph, named for the eighteenth-century Swiss mathematician Leonhard Euler.

Diagram 4.3

Proposition	Graph
All P is K	

By means of the diagram given above, we immediately grasp that each and every thing which is a pianist, that is, the class represented by the rectangled P, is related to each and every thing which is a keyboardist, or the class represented by the rectangled K, and that the relation is expressed through "is." The relation expressed through "is," in this case, can be defined as "is included in." The modified Euler graph representing this relation illustrates it by means of the geometric relation "is inside of."

"All pianists are keyboardists" is, then, our first premise. Let us suppose that the investigation of our deduction is to conclude what the relation is between pianists and artists. We then add two additional premises to the first, these two being "All keyboardists are musicians" and "All musicians are artists." By employing the propositional and graphical conventions used above, we can then represent the complete deduction with its conclusion. Using the three premises in their original propositional formulations, we would begin with the following.

Syllogism 4

All pianists are keyboardists.
All keyboardists are musicians.
All musicians are artists.

_____

Therefore: All pianists are artists.

Extending our earlier use of abbrevations, this deduction can be reduced to the following.

Diagram 4.4

All P is K
All K is M
All M is A

_____

Therefore: All P is A

Its graphical equivalent, then, is given in diagram 4.5, below. If you take care to note how, at each step along the way, the relevant rectangles interlock with one another in an ascending order according to the size of the class they represent, you will see how, if the premises in fact be true, the conclusion would be utterly inescapable.

Proposition	Graph

Diagram 4.5

All P is K

All K is M

All M is A

Therefore,
All P is A

The important aspect of this illustration, of course, is *not* the actual everyday contents of these classes, but rather the manner in which these classes are brought into relations with one another to produce a valid *form* of argument. Whether or not the argument itself is sound depends additionally, of course, on the truth of the premises. This kind of argument in the logical relations of classes is of the type that can be treated completely and correctly using the kind of logic machine proposed by Peirce and his student and colleague Allan Marquand. It can do this because it relies on and operates according to what is termed an *algorithm,* which is defined as "a mechanical procedure for carrying out, in a finite number of steps, a computation that leads from certain types of data to certain types of results" (see Brody 1967). It is the algorithm that defines the limits of a machine's computational sophistication, the limit of its "fixed method," the limit beyond which our creative faculties hold sway. To examine and illustrate more clearly what an algorithm is and how it works, we will consider the remarkable story of Peirce and Marquand's early computer design. (For a fuller account, see Ketner with Stewart 1984.)

Allan Marquand (1853–1924) was the son of the art collector and philanthropist Henry G. Marquand, and perhaps the most prominent of Peirce's students during his time at Johns Hopkins University. Peirce was a part-time faculty member in logic at the new university from 1879 through 1884 and concurrently maintained a full-time position as assistant at the U.S. Coast and Geodetic Survey. The title "assistant" required more responsibility and authority than we would, these days, ordinarily associate with it. He held the Coast Survey position from 1859 until his resignation in 1891. While at Hopkins he was active as well in the areas of mathematics, psychology, and philosophy. However, it is Peirce's activities in logic, especially with Marquand, that concern us here.

Marquand was a fellow in philosophy and ethics at Hopkins until the completion of his doctorate in 1880. His essay on the logic of

Philodemus was written under Peirce's supervision and was the only doctoral dissertation ever completed under Peirce's direction. *Studies in Logic by Members of the Johns Hopkins University*, which appeared in 1883 under Peirce's editorship, included the introduction to Marquand's dissertation, entitled "The Logic of the Epicureans," as the first part. In 1881 Marquand joined the faculty at Princeton as Tutor in Latin and lecturer in Logic. In 1883, probably as a result of a dispute with the university president, Marquand changed his position at Princeton by becoming professor of art and archaeology, a position he held until his death.

While still a student at Hopkins, Marquand had been directed, by Peirce, to the task of developing an improved version of William Stanley Jevons's mechanical instrument for performing syllogistic reasoning, his "Logical Piano," so called because, to use an analogy with modern computers, its "keyboard" resembled a section of a piano keyboard. Marquand contributed heavily to the first issue of *Studies in Logic,* including an essay entitled "A Machine for Producing Syllogistic Variations" and the following "Note on an Eight Term Logical Machine." From these contributions it is clear that Marquand had already devised three types of aids for logical computation. The first such device consisted of logical diagrams or graphs; the second was a mechanically crank-operated realization of these diagrams; and the third improved the Jevons machine, providing operation by depression of keys. Peirce was completely familiar with these developments and certainly had the upgraded Jevons device in mind when writing the "logical machine" entry for Whitney's *Dictionary and Cyclopedia.*

Logical machine, a machine which, being fed with premises, produces the necessary conclusions from them. The earliest instrument of this kind was the demonstrator of Charles, third Earl Stanhope: the most perfect is that of Professor Allan Marquand, which gives all inferences turning upon the logical relations of classes. The value of logical machines seems to lie in their showing how far reasoning is a mechanical process, and how far it calls for acts of observation. Calculating machines are specialized logical machines. (Peirce 1889: 3560)

But what, exactly, was Peirce referring to when noting Marquand's "most perfect" machine? James Mark Baldwin reported the important third development by Marquand, the improved or upgraded version of Jevons's Logical Piano, in his *Dictionary of Philosophy and Psychology* under the entry "Logical Machine." He also mentioned a crucial fourth development, one that, by involving electricity, departed quite radically from its predecessors.

In 1882 Marquand constructed from an ordinary hotel annunciator another machine in which all the combinations are visible at the outset, and the inconsistent combinations are concealed from view as the premises are impressed upon the keys. He also had designs made by means of which the same operations could be accomplished by means of electro-magnets. (Baldwin 1902/II: 2930)

Did Peirce have, in addition to his thorough acquaintance with the improved Logical Piano, knowledge of such designs involving electromagnets when reporting in the *Century Dictionary and Cyclopedia* on Marquand's "most perfect" logical machine?

Marquand published on the subject of his advancement of the Logical Piano in the *Proceedings of the American Academy of Arts and Sciences for 1885–1886*, naming the essay "A New Logical Machine." He had presented this paper before the AAAS on 11 November 1885, apparently being disappointed with its reception. In a letter dated 30 December 1886, Peirce encouraged Marquand's will to learn and urged him to continue improving his logic machine. In his letter, Peirce suggested the introduction of a new component in the design of logic machines, a component that would quickly lead to a design, as reported by Baldwin, involving electromagnets. The component was electricity:

I think you ought to return to the problem, especially as it is by no means hopeless to expect to make a machine for really very difficult mathematical problems. But you would have to proceed step by step. I think electricity would be the best thing to rely on.

Diagram 4.6

Peirce's hand-drawn circuits

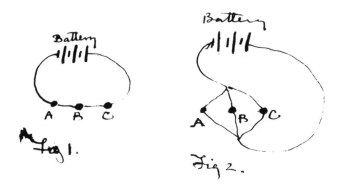

(*Papers of Allan Marquand, Manuscript Division, Department of Rare Books and Special Collections. Courtesy Princeton University Libraries*)

Let A, B, C be three keys or other points where the circuit may be open or closed. As in Fig. 1, there is a circuit only if *all* are closed; in Fig. 2 there is a circuit if *any one* is closed. This is like multiplication & addition in logic. (Peirce 1886, using his hand-drawn figures)

These diagrams of series and parallel electrical circuits make possible and indeed illustrate the inevitability of properly performed logical multiplication and addition: the conjunction "A · B"; the disjunction "A v B" (see diagram 4.1). Either or both relations may represent for us propositions, beliefs, and knowledge items, and either or both relations may clearly be instantiated in electrical circuitry and computing machines, as in Shannon's analogs of fifty years later (see Shannon 1938). So, clearly, some parts of our knowledge that are deductive in character can be instantiated in machines. But this is quite different from concluding that because *some parts* of our knowledge are machine computable, *all parts* must be.

Peirce's remarkable letter lay in the Allan Marquand Papers at Princeton University Library, apparently unnoticed, until its discovery around 1970 by Professor Preston Tuttle. In addition to this unique letter there is another, even more fascinating piece of evidence on the subject of Peirce, Marquand, and logic machines in the Marquand Papers at Princeton. This is a design of the type using electromagnets that, according to Baldwin, Marquand "had made." This electromagnetic design was first noticed at Princeton by Professor Alonzo Church, about 1950. Historical evidence surrounding this diagram indicates that it was drawn up about 1887 and that its author was Peirce (see diagram 4.7).

This diagram represents a proposed electromechanical machine that performs, by purely algorithmic means, deductions in the logical relation of classes involving up to four terms. It exhibits four basic types of components: electromagnets, circuit keys for the introduction of premises, an operations switch, and a power supply consisting of two batteries. Consistent with Baldwin's remarks and with the instructions for operation found on the original drawing, we would begin logical operations with this machine with "all the [logical] combinations [being] visible" (Baldwin 1902/II: 29). These logical combinations, each four letters in length, would be matched to the electromagnets according to the grid of exhaustive possibilities implicit in the lettering on the diagram, where uppercase and lowercase letters represent the truth and falsity, respectively, of each of the four terms. The "visible combinations," to begin, would look like this.

Diagram 4.7

ABCD	AbCD	aBCD	abCD
ABCd	AbCd	aBCd	abCd
ABcD	AbcD	aBcD	abcD
ABcd	Abcd	aBcd	abcd

The design with electromagnets looks like this:

Diagram 4.8

Circuit diagram for electromagnetic logical machine

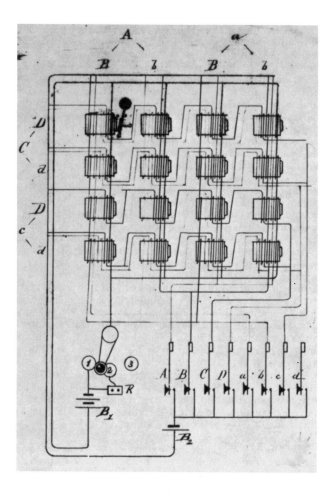

(Papers of Allan Marquand, Manuscript Division, Department of Rare Books
and Special Collections. Courtesy Princeton University Libraries)

Premises are introduced by means of the circuit keys, which are lettered, as in diagram 4.7, above, to handle these four terms and their negations. As premises are thus entered, the inconsistent logical combinations that result are, by actions of the electromagnets, removed from view. So, for example, successful entry of the premise "All A are B" would leave in view only those combinations with 'A' and 'B' in them. A second premise "All B are C" would retain in the machine's memory only those combinations containing 'B' and 'C'. Successive entries would rely on the same principles.

Let us now suppose that we wish to work a four-term categorical deduction of the type initiated earlier with the premise "All pianists are keyboardists." Here, however, we will use the four terms A, B, C, and D instead of our earlier abbreviations. Our three premises are, then:

Diagram 4.9

All A is B
All B is C
All C is D

Our aim is to discern what logical relation may obtain between classes represented by the terms A and D. These premises are entered in discrete steps, with each term or variable handled in turn. After all three premises have been entered and the attendant inconsistent logical combinations, which in this case means any combination containing at least one lowercase letter, concealed, the result of our mechanized working of a four-term categorical deduction is the valid conclusion "All A is D."

We see that by observing the conventions for entry of premises and thus setting into action the matrix of the proposed machine, the result is completely, precisely, and *repeatably* determined by finite, algorithmic means. The elements with which this deductive activity began were, of course, our premises for a four-term categorical deduction.

This is, then, an example from the collection or set of argument forms that the Peirce-Marquand machine *can* execute. Especially important is the procedure or method embodied in the actual physical arrangement of the machine with its entry keys, electromagnets, and such by which this activity is carried out. This method mechanically, deterministically, and repeatably proceeds from premises to conclusions by means of a recipe, or finite set of instructions. Such a set of instructions is termed an algorithm. And again, *some* parts of our knowledge may indeed be instantiated in machines driven by algorithms, but this does not soundly argue that *all* our knowledge may be reduced to algorithms. The machine driven by an algorithm is limited in ways that the active mind is not. Now the active mind may, of course, make mistakes that the computer would not, but the active mind's limits to truth or error will not be set by an algorithm, as they explicitly are in computing machines.

The fact that deductive logic is thus machine computable by algorithmic means illustrates yet again that this adjunct method of acquiring and developing human knowledge involves matters independent of our subjective views. Deductive validity is an *objective* state of things. It is *real* and, as Peirce put it, "therefore independent of the vagaries of me and you" (*CP* 5.311). In this same objective sense, both the formal and informal fallacies we shall see in chapter 5 are important cutting or filtering tools in pragmatic investigations.

5

Deduction and Induction

■ *Deductive reasoning has many forms and many possible defects as well. Our logic of events and our pragmatic ethics of the mind depend heavily on both deductive and inductive reasoning. In the light of rationalism and empiricism, as espoused by Descartes and Hume, the following question emerges: Can knowledge be derived from our reasoning alone, or does our sense experience play the predominant role?*

E NEED TO consider two additional forms of syllogism, as well as two examples of arguments in *modus ponens* and *modus tollens*. All four of these examples of deductive reasoning are drawn from propositional logic, and all also exhibit an objective character; that is, the conclusions drawn by proper use of these logical forms of argument are independent of our subjective views.

The disjunctive syllogism, in which one premise is a disjunctive proposition, namely, an "either . . . or . . ." statement, is a deductive form you are already at least partially familiar with. The form of disjunctive syllogism allows for, but is not limited to, the theoretical and practical resolution of a contradiction, like the pairing of incompatible statements about human beings and machines found in chapter 4. Its applications are available for a range of problems broader than simple, formal contradiction. All disjunctive syllogisms demand a definite

choice between two alternatives forced by the "either . . . or . . ." construction. For example, the disjunctive proposition "Either my cowboy boots
are black or they are red," a statement easily used in a disjunctive syllogism,
is clearly different from the humans-versus-machines pairing that we examined in chapter 4. The disjunctive syllogism, then, has two, and only
two, possibly valid forms. Retaining the conventions 'v' = 'or' and '~'
= 'not', and acknowledging the abbreviations 'H' and 'M' for "human
beings" and "machines," respectively, you can fill in or reconstitute
these stripped-down versions of the disjunctive syllogism to produce
actual examples of this process of deductive reasoning.

Diagram 5.1

H v M

~H

_____

M

OR

Diagram 5.2

H v M

~M

_____

H

The above diagrams read as follows: "Something is either H or M. It
is not H. Therefore, it is M." Or "Something is either H or M. It is
not M. Therefore, it is H.

Notice that the second premise, here a single term, is always negative and, by being negative, cancels out one of the two terms in the
first premise when the two premises are combined. The remaining
term from this canceling out makes for the conclusion. The same requirements concerning truth, validity, and soundness apply to the disjunctive syllogism as to the categorical syllogism; only thoroughgoing

truth in premise materials combined with strict validity of form will produce a sound argument, the kind of argument whose conclusion is a matter of uncompromising and objective certainty.

If you are willing to apply a bit of ordinary experience and some self-critical creativity to these valid forms of disjunctive, deductive argumentation, you will be able to construct examples from immediate experience that will demonstrate the everyday value of this syllogism. Do not worry if your illustrative examples seem unimportant or even silly; just be sure the form is correct. The *practical* importance of an argument will depend on its real life circumstances, and its practical importance may therefore vary. For example, "I *either* eat frozen yogurt *or* a chicken sandwich for my lunch" may seem completely arbitrary or unimportant to you at the moment you wish and will to act on this disjunction. But if your living disjunction is "*either* I eat a chicken sandwich *and* frozen yogurt *or* I eat nothing at all," and perhaps for several days, then the practical and conceivable consequences of your argument could be crucial to you.

The next deductive form on our schedule is the pure hypothetical syllogism, so named because each premise and conclusion are hypothetical or conditional statements. Such hypothetical or conditional statements invite us to speculate about or to predict future events based on the relation of cause and effect. Thus, such explanatory predictions use the "If . . . then . . ." construction. This syllogism has one and only one valid form, as in the following example:

Diagram 5.3

If it is raining, then the street will be wet.
If the street is wet, then it will be slippery.

Therefore, if it is raining, then the street will be slippery.

Notice that the internal form of this syllogism is exactly the same as that for the selected categorical syllogism reduced in diagram 4.2 of chapter 4. Thus, the first term of the first premise returns as the first term of the conclusion; the second term of the second premise returns as the second term of the conclusion; and the term used to conclude the first premise relates diagonally to the first term of the second but does not recur in the conclusion at all. Also, the issues of truth, validity, and soundness, discussed in chapter 4, retain their former characters and relations.

The final two deductive forms to be considered here are known as *modus ponens,* and *modus tollens.* Each deals, in its own way, with the relation of cause and effect; each has its own, uniquely valid form; and the connections within each between truth, validity, and soundness are also still in play.

Using as the first premise "If it is raining, then the street will be wet," diagram 5.4 represents a visual version of an argument in *modus ponens.* This argument outlines the following cause and effect relation. The first premise claims that if the cause in question, "rain," is present, then the predicted effect, "wet street," will be the result. The second premise informs us that the cause, "rain," is indeed present, and so the conclusion, unexceptionally, presents the predicted effect, "wet street."

Diagram 5.4

If it is raining, then the street will be wet.
It is raining.

Therefore, the street will be wet.

We can abbreviate the whole matter with 'R' (rain) representing the antecedent or beginning part of the premise and with 'W' (wet) standing for the consequent or concluding part of the premise. The reduced or stripped-down version of this example would then look like diagram 5.5. Just as one would expect for such an expression of the cause and effect relation, the first term of the first premise reappears, alone, as the second premise, while the second term of the first premise returns as the conclusion.

Diagram 5.5

If R, then W

R

———————

W

Modus ponens is also a formal expression of what is known as a *sufficient condition*. That is, the causal agent in this scheme, namely, the action summarized by the antecedent term 'R', is all that is required for the subsequent appearance of the effect, namely, the resulting event summarized by the consequent term signified by 'W'. We then say that this condition R is a sufficient condition for the appearance of W. Obviously, there could be any number of sufficient conditions that could function as the antecedent in this argument. A turned-on fire hydrant, wasteful lawn watering, a wrecked beer truck, or any number of other circumstances could function just as well as the causative agent or sufficient condition in this deduction. It is not at all unusual to find a number of sufficient conditions for the appearance of a certain single effect. And simply to claim that the absence of a particular sufficient condition will prevent the appearance of the consequent effect commits the *formal* fallacy of denying the antecedent.

For many, *modus tollens* is a more difficult business to understand. In this instance we begin with the reduced version of this argument employing only the letters 'R' (the condition of rain) and 'C' (the condition of clouds), with their negations.

Diagram 5.6

If R, then C

~C

———————

~R

Notice here that both the second premise and the conclusion are negative, that the second premise, again a single term, is drawn from the *second* or consequent part of the first premise, while the conclusion derives from the first or antecedent part of the first premise. Diagram 5.7 fleshes out the argument.

Diagram 5.7

If it is to rain, then we must have clouds present.
NO clouds are present.

_____

Therefore, it *WILL NOT* rain.

Pause for a moment and look at this example a little more closely. Obviously, rain does not cause clouds, so a sufficient condition is not expressed by this hypothetical or conditional statement we take as our first premise. But is it not in fact the case that, should we lack the presence of clouds, we know as a matter of *necessity* that rain cannot form? This is why the consequent of an argument in *modus tollens* is said to express not a sufficient condition, but a *necessary condition,* which by itself will not cause the effect we may be interested in, but whose absence will guarantee that this effect will not occur. It is stated in this negative, and probably initially confusing form, because there is no better way to demonstrate something as a necessary condition than to show that its absence, expressed as its negation, necessarily precludes the appearance of its antecedent companion. Notice, also, how clouds alone cannot function as a sufficient condition for the appearance of rain. In fact, to so claim would commit the formal fallacy of affirming the consequent. But also notice how clouds—accompanied by certain conditions of humidity, atmospheric pressure, temperature, and the like—could, as a group, function as a single sufficient condition made up of a number of subsidiary and distinct conditions.

This brings us, then, to a pair of useful generalizations about these two forms of argument concerning sufficient and necessary conditions and their causal implications. (1) The realization of a sufficient condition, expressed as the antecedent of an argument in *modus ponens,* will cause the appearance of the consequential effect, while (2) the lack of realization of a necessary condition, expressed as the consequent of an argument in *modus tollens,* will prevent the appearance of its antecedent companion. Thus, the effective expression of a sufficient condition will reveal the workings of a cause and effect relation, while the effective suppression of a necessary condition will break up any possible cause and effect relation that may have been possible or implied. Careful application of these two argument forms shows them to be rather reliable but, of course, not guaranteed or infallible tools for revealing the functioning of sufficient and necessary conditions.

Some cause and effect arguments express only a necessary condition as in diagram 5.7, above, and some express only a sufficient condition as in diagram 5.4. Perhaps unsurprisingly, some express *both* a sufficient and a necessary condition. For example, if every time I drive onto an interstate highway I wish to reach a speed of 65 m.p.h. as promptly as the traffic demands and allows, I must apply increasing downward force on the accelerator until those rates of acceleration and speed are reached. If my intent is to reach that speed exactly, my pressure on the accelerator must be nothing less than the necessary condition for increasing speed to 65, and nothing more than the sufficient condition of increasing force will, in turn, allow for and guarantee the suitable level of acceleration and speed. A little ingenuity and a bit of ordinary experience will allow you to find further examples of all three expressions of (1) sufficient, (2) necessary, and (3) both sufficient and necessary conditions. Just be sure to remember that only sound deductive arguments produce the sorts of guaranteed or certain conclusions for which deductive reasoning is known.

Deductive reasoning is often, and rightly, associated with the seventeenth-century French thinker René Descartes (1596–1650), frequently referred to as the father of modern philosophy. Descartes felt certain about a number of things having to do with methods of acquiring and developing knowledge, and it will be helpful for us to become acquainted with each of these.

First, continuing the tradition of rationalism that extended back two millennia to Plato, Descartes had grave doubts that sense experience by itself could have any value in the acquisition and development of human knowledge:

> All that up to the present time I have accepted as most true and certain I have learned either from the senses or through the senses; but it is sometimes proved to me that these senses are deceptive, and it is wiser not to trust entirely to any thing by which we have once been deceived. (Haldane and Ross 1911: 1:145).

Descartes thus believed that knowledge could be gained in an "a priori" or deductive manner, independent of or *prior* to sense experience. Such rudimentary knowledge, known indubitably by intuition, could form a foundation from which, deductively, all human knowledge could be derived. Intuition was a highly important factor in Descartes's system: "This evidence and certitude . . . which belongs to intuition is required not only in the enunciation of propositions, but also in discursive reasoning of whatever sort" (Haldane and Ross 1911: 1:7). Deduction, capable of producing certainty, will, given the right rudimentary materials, then provide for absolutely secure human knowledge.

Descartes thought that by winnowing out all his mistaken beliefs, in fact by eliminating any belief that he could even reasonably doubt or be skeptical of, he would reach the needed rudiments. His winnowing technique was systematic doubt; his rudiment was a kind of self-awareness expressed in his famous pronouncement *cogito, ergo sum*, "I think, therefore I am." In his language, "I am, I exist, is necessarily true each time that I pronounce it, or that I mentally conceive it" (Haldane and Ross 1911: 1:150). Descartes then used this truth as an *axiom:* a primitive truth that we not only do not try to prove, but that, due to its genuinely primitive nature, we cannot prove even if we desire to. Descartes claims to know that he has arrived at this indubitable truth of self-awareness because (1) he cannot rationally doubt it, and (2) it is an idea to him that is "clear and distinct." What does this phrase "clear and distinct" mean?

I call that clear which is present and apparent to an attentive mind, in the same way as we assert that we see objects clearly when, being present to the regarding eye, they operate upon it with sufficient strength. But the distinct is that which is so precise and different from all other objects that it contains within itself nothing but what is clear (Haldane and Ross 1955: 1:237).

And because this axiom is known independently of sense experience, by an intuition that confirms itself by being clear and distinct, Descartes is committed to the doctrine of the superiority of innate ideas. In other words, in any truly rationalistic scheme like Descartes's, innate or inborn ideas and knowledge will always take precedence over any ideas or knowledge acquired through sense experience.

So, for Descartes, our knowledge develops as we combine the right axiom(s) with a process of deductive reasoning that includes the operation of intuition. If all this seems rather mathematical, it is not by accident. Axioms and deductive reasoning are defining components of mathematical systems like Euclidean geometry. Descartes thus attempted to form a deductive, mathematical model for human knowledge.

But of course the very certainty that deduction provides is also its great limitation. Do we really know only what we think we know with such absolute certainty? Do life and certain knowledge really fall into such neat little schemes of certainty, lack of doubts, and guarantees that deduction, in its limited way, seems so preoccupied with? Of course not. But deduction does have two enormous values for us in an uncertain world, a world that demands from us both creativity and experimentation. First, deduction can be enormously helpful in organizing and clarifying life experiences we are already familiar with. It can help us identify and give sharper definition to some of the seemingly recurring patterns in experience. By this means, deduction can, if approached undogmatically, help us to understand better our present or "just past" experience and, by further analogical application, even give us something of a *seeming* glimpse into the future. But this latter business is always fraught with peril, because deduction in and of itself has, strictly considered, no ability to predict. When we do predict, when we confront ourselves with the patently *un*certain future, deduction can, however, give us a technique for eliminating mistakes and errors in our beliefs and knowledge once they have actually arrived. The business of prediction and probability, the business that brings us to the point in our knowledge where deductive elimination of mistakes and errors can occur, is induction.

Of the several topics sometimes joined under the subject of induction, for the present we will only be concerned with one. This topic, however, is probably the one that is the most basic of all these various topics and is a commonplace in our lives. It involves analogy, generalization, and prediction, and is an example of what is sometimes known as *induction by simple enumeration.*

Induction, in the sense used here, still retains the basic structure of any legitimate argument form, including deductive forms. The internal components of an inductive argument, however, do not demand quite the same degree of precision in their placement as that required in deduction. This should come as no surprise, given that induction does not and cannot make the claims of certainty that deduction can and does make. By using induction, if we assume the evidence or premises to be true and we employ the best analogical or inductive reasoning we can, our conclusion is made *probable*, and perhaps even astonishingly probable, but never quite certain.

Consider a simple example from common experience of analogical or inductive reasoning. Suppose I hold up my left hand, fingers outstretched and with its palm facing you. Now additionally suppose that I place my right hand against my left, palms together so that you now see not the palm of my left hand but the back of my right hand, and further suppose that my right thumb is folded in and concealed be-

tween the two palms. What do you now see, overall? You see one figure, composed of my two hands arranged in such a way that the general pattern made by my left hand, in the background, seems perfectly
duplicated by my right hand in the foreground, except that you see
the palm side of my left thumb quite clearly, but you cannot see my
right thumb at all. The mind demands almost instinctively to know if
the missing thumb is going to appear and thereby complete and fill
out the overall pattern. This demand is, in fact, an inductive inference,
in three parts: (1) you have collected from the past and unconsciously
placed in your memory an enormous number of individual cases
where you have observed that people have two hands and that these
hands are roughly symmetrical with each other; (2) noticing that this
present case bears similarities to past ones, you predict that the apparent analogical similarity between past and present will be carried
forward and completed in the future; and (3) observing that the present case is indeed analogically consistent with past experience, eventually confirmed by the appearance of the missing thumb, you generalize or predict for general purposes that, based on past experience
and on the consistency of this new experience with the past, it is quite
likely or highly probable that any new person you inspect for these
manual characteristics will, indeed, have them. Unlike deduction,
however, certainty in this conclusion cannot be obtained. No amount
of past information, however large or internally consistent or agreeable with new cases or specimens, can render an inductive conclusion
certain. But as with deduction, we look for a clear "match" between
true evidence and a properly conducted reasoning process to yield a
conclusion.

More exactly, if we assume that the premises in an inductive procedure are true and that the conclusion will be rendered probable, we
say the inductive process or the induction overall is a strong one. If we
combine actually true premises with a strong inductive procedure, we
have a cogent argument. These forms, as we shall find, do indeed have
their parallels or analogues with deductive procedures. Another, more
involved example of induction will help illustrate these points and will

acquaint us with some of the more technical aspects involved in inductions, including the notion of an "explanatory hypothesis."

Let us suppose that instead of sitting around staring at our hands we have been asked to perform a service for zoological classification, that is, we are to come up with the best and most complete description we can for the class of animals known as "mammals." Using a rough generalization from our collective experience, we arrive at a predictive or hypothetical explanation of what characteristics we generally expect mammals to have. Our rough hypothesis, our initial abduction that actual experience can confirm or reject or even ignore at any moment, is that mammals seem to share four characteristics: they are warm-blooded, they have hair, they feed their young with self-produced milk, and they bring their offspring into the world by using live birth, rather than by laying eggs. We can abbreviate these characteristics thus: 'W' represents "warm-blooded," 'H' represents "have hair," 'M' represents the factor of milk, and 'L' represents the factor of live birth. Let us further suppose that, while the first three characteristics may be confirmed rather quickly in any given instance, confirmation of factor L must be waited for. Thus, from an initially inspected group of animals of whatever size in our initial abduction, we form the narrower and thus more easily tested explanatory hypothesis "Mammals that have characteristics W, H, M will, we predict, with a degree of probability, have characteristic L." Further, "Those specimens with all four characteristics support our hypothesis."

Now, what do we do with this hypothesis, this result of predesignation, which may be nothing more than a lucky guess or may even be partially or completely erroneous? We test it against that very phenomenon that it is supposed to explain, namely, as much of the animal kingdom as possible. This is pragmatism in action, and this factor of testability is crucial to it. In this same spirit of pragmatism, the pedigree of our initial hypothesis is, logically, irrelevant. Now, of course, irrational considerations in the formulation of it, logical flaws or subjective biases, and the like, might, from their past records in other similar or analogous experiments, warn us against certain seeming missteps along the way. Being thus experienced may allow us to practice a certain economy in our methods, but the basic question about this or any other explanatory hypothesis remains exactly the same from the pragmatic point of view: *will it survive being tested?*

What should the test in the illustration be? The test should be examining how this explanatory hypothesis survives in future trials against new specimens. Let us suppose that our actual testing procedure involves our traveling all over the globe, examining as many creatures as we can find, all the while comparing our hypothesis against what we actually see. As our test proceeds, we begin to suspect that new specimens readily exhibiting three of the four characteristics listed in our hypothesis will also exhibit the fourth. In other words, for each new specimen examined, we expect an analogy, an *inductive* analogy, with past specimens to hold. Let us simplify the matter for the sake of a clear illustration. Let us suppose that the characteristic that will complete the analogy in any given case, rather like the appearance of the thumb in the earlier illustration, is the characteristic of producing offspring by live birth. Past experience, perhaps rather unorganized, haphazard, or even misleading, which we lump together here as 'X', has led us quite tentatively or cautiously to expect, as our explanatory hypothesis or 'EH', the following.

Diagram 5.8

As the result of X, EH = W, H, M, and L
— narrowed to —
where W, H, and M are found, L is likely to be found.

Let us term our first studiously examined new specimen X+1, which we immediately see has the first three of the characteristics but which provides no immediate evidence of the fourth. EH tested against X+1, at this point, would look like this.

Diagram 5.9

$$X \text{ or } EH = W, H, M, \text{ and } L$$
$$X+1 = W, H, M, \text{ and } ?$$

Now, upon closer examination of the specimen and, of course, after having waited for future events to take their course, let us suppose that, indeed, live birth is an observed characteristic of X+1. Now our test of EH against X+1 fills out and becomes like the following.

*Diagram
5.10*

$$X \text{ or } EH = W, H, M, \text{ and } L$$
$$X+1 = W, H, M, \text{ and } L$$

The now-complete agreement between X or EH, on the one hand, and X+1, on the other, may be observed. We may now use X+1 as our experimental model, looking further for others of its kind that either do include property 'L', thus confirming EH further, or that *do not* include property 'L', thus not confirming EH. In other words, using X+1 as our model, we will continue to look for inductive analogies between X+1 and subsequent occurrences X+2, X+3, and so forth, in the as yet unknown future. Of course, we are in fact comparing each new specimen against our original EH, but as a practical matter of economy of research we look for inductive analogies amongst the specimens themselves. In so doing, we wish to build up a suitably large sample of empirical specimens that, collectively, either confirm or contradict EH. And of course we know that any future specimen that matches in the relevant characteristics with X+1 will also confirm EH.

After building up a substantial group of such cases that are consistent with one another and that seem to confirm our explanatory hypothesis, that is, after our sample size is large enough, we may inductively generalize to the effect that there is a clear probability that *all* animals having characteristics W, H, and M, will also have characteristic L. Obviously, having examined only two or three animals that happen to agree with our hypothesis is not enough evidence to generalize from, and to generalize in that way commits the informal fallacy of hasty generalization.

But for the moment let us assume that the number of examples and successful inductive analogies in our sample is enormous. Let us assume, for the sake of the illustration, that we have examined specimens sufficient to list specimen X+10,000 as consistent with its predecessors. So now we have an enormous sample size, complete consistency of inductive analogies within it, and, consequently, a very powerful generalization to be made. Should we cease our labors and simply conclude, "Oh well, it is a *certainty* now that no significant exceptions to our explanatory hypothesis will ever be found"? The methods of dogmatism might so conclude, but pragmatism says, strictly speaking, that you may never so conclude and cease inquiry. Why? Because any predictive, inductive explaining or even guessing about the future must, for now, remain only, in Peirce's expression, "a mere Maybe" (*NEM,* vol.3, sec. 2: 869–870).

The eighteenth-century Scottish philosopher David Hume (1711–1776) had something important to say about induction and its predictive capacity, something we should all take care to remember. Hume, unlike Descartes, believed that the source of all human knowledge is to be found in the empirical realm of sense experience. Hume thus continues the rational tradition, extending back to Aristotle, known as empiricism. For Hume, sense experiences or "impressions" lead to our simple ideas, and our own creativity can manipulate these simple ideas into complex ones. But however complex an idea may become in our knowledge, it can always, eventually, be traced backwards to an original sense experience. Hume uses our understanding of the notion of "golden mountain" as an illustration; each of the two component parts of this complex idea can, as simple ideas themselves, be traced backwards to a corresponding sense perception of a color and an object. In Hume's view, if we suspect that an idea is somehow artificially produced without reference to sense experience, "We need but inquire, *from what impression is that supposed idea derived?* And if it be impossible to assign any, this will serve to confirm our suspicion" (Selby-Bigge 1975: 22).

Thus, in Hume's scheme of things, human knowledge is an a posteriori, a "post-experience," matter. For Hume, our knowledge does not rely, as it does with Descartes, on innate ideas, but rather on ideas *acquired* via experience. Such "matters of fact," as Hume termed them, are dealt with by means of inductive or "experimental" reasoning, while "relations of ideas," as Hume named them, are managed by means of deductive or "demonstrative" reasoning. Hume observes:

Of [the deductive] kind are the sciences of geometry, algebra, and arithmetic, and in short every affirmation which is either intuitively or demonstratively certain. *That the square of the hypotenuse is equal to the square of the two sides* is a proposition which expresses a relation between these figures. . . . Matters of fact, which are the second objects of human reason, are not ascertained in the same manner; . . . The contrary of every matter of fact is still possible. . . . All reasoning concerning matters of fact seems to be founded on the relation of *Cause and Effect.* . . . From causes which appear *similar* we expect similar effects. This is the sum of all our experimental conclusions. (Selby-Bigge 1975: 25, 26; 36).

And while we trust in and use inductive reasoning constantly, Hume believed that any attempted rational proof of it would inevitably force the reasoner into a circular argument, namely, one where the seemingly novel conclusion appears, often disguised, as an already accepted premise. This is an important point that bears some elaboration.

Briefly put, Hume's problem with induction comes to the following. Induction deals, as we know, with predicting how the relation of cause and effect, observed in past cases, will play itself out in future cases of similar sorts. Now if we wish to attempt a rational proof of induction, to what two faculties would we have to appeal? First, we would have to rely on our powers of observation, and second, we would have to rely just as much on our powers of memory of past observations. Neither observation nor memory can function reliably for us unless the relation of cause and effect is already *in play* in our experience, but the relation of cause and effect is the very thing we wish to demonstrate. Thus, Hume claims that any attempted proof of cause and effect relations requires the use of memory and observation but that these elements of "proof" themselves already rely on the existence of the very relation we wish to use them to prove! Thus, as Hume says, this sort of arguing to prove what is already assumed true is indeed unacceptable. We term this the informal fallacy of circular reasoning or begging the question. To try to prove that future events will be like those of past experience where we have always noticed certain "causes" always leading to certain "effects" will, for Hume, "be evidently going in a circle and taking for granted the very point in question" (Selby-Bigge 1975: 35–36). The "may-be's" of the future thus cannot make for present certainties.

For the present moment, then, we cannot convert inductive generalization into deductive certainty. This is a logical reason why inquiry or pragmatic investigation cannot come to a stop. Is there a practical reason as well, one we can perhaps more immediately use? Peirce made some remarks in his 1892 article for *The Monist,* entitled "The Doctrine of Necessity Examined," that provide us with an informative transition to a completely *practical* reason for not thus blocking the road to inquiry.

. . . the conclusions of science make no pretense to being more than probable . . . [;] a probable inference can at most only suppose something to be most frequently, or otherwise approximately, true, but never that anything is precisely true without exception throughout the universe. (CP 6.39)

The completely practical reason for continuing our classificational efforts is that, if we persist long enough in our investigations, we come upon a creature that satisfies the first three conditions we have accepted as defining characteristics of mammalian life, *but not the fourth.* The creature, of course, is the platypus. Because the platypus, mammalian in most respects, lays eggs instead of producing live births and thus presents us with a problem for our inductive procedure. Where 'E' represents "lays eggs," if our platypus were example X+10,001, the attempt to complete an inductive analogy with its immediate predecessor would become disjointed.

Diagram 5.11

$$X + 10,000 = W, H, M, \text{ and } L$$
$$\text{BUT}$$
$$X + 10,001 = W, H, M, \text{ and } E!$$

The match between these two specimens is not satisfactory to us, based on our wealth of past experience and the inductive power it provides. Because the platypus goes against or runs counter to all the examples we have examined thus far, and goes against or runs counter to our explanatory hypothesis, it is termed an inductive counterexample. Such dilemmas between our predictive explanations and that which we seek to explain bring forth one of the most basic issues for scientific or pragmatic method. The issue can be put in question form: Which shall give ground when our theories or explanatory hypotheses do not quite fit that which they were supposed to explain—our theories or that which our theories explain, our hypotheses or the world? In our present case, of course, we simply produce a revised explanatory hypothesis that acknowledges either the laying of eggs or the giving of live birth as mammalian characteristics, and continue on with our investigations. But there are two other alternatives that are not so easily accommodated.

The first alternative to mere revision introduces dogmatism, at least, or, in extreme cases, an irrational or even insane disconnection from the world. It demands that the world change to fit our hypothesis. The second alternative requires eliminating, in a certain, decisive, *deductive* way, our erroneous beliefs. If we really do suppose that we can change the world merely to fit our theories about it, then we will quickly find ourselves propping up all sorts of embarrassing assumptions by ad hoc means. The history of medicine, as we know, provides a clear example of this in the now-debunked humoral theory of disease. In the end, the practice was given up because the explanatory hypothesis it was based on was just plain wrong. And as for the deductive elimination of it, investigators found that this theory was not just inductively or probably wrong, but that it was deductively and certainly wrong. In that instance, the type and number of counterexamples were of a sort so overwhelming, so contradictory to experience as to require not simply attempts at successful modification of the hypothesis but the complete discarding of it altogether. On the other hand, the germ theory was and remains inductively or probably right, having not been deductively eliminated.

So it would appear that our explanatory hypotheses versus that which they are to explain are, by analogy, rather like biological species versus their environments: some will survive and prosper without much challenge for the time being, while others will have characteristics allowing them to exhibit modifications that make them more suitable in important respects, while still others will simply go extinct. The process itself, then, is self-correcting. This is a completely pragmatic way to view how we acquire and develop our knowledge: our developments of knowledge are clearly analogous to the processes of biological evolution.

The analogues of truth, validity, and soundness—the tenets of deduction—are, in induction, truth, strength of argument, and overall cogency. That is, again, if the premises of an inductive argument are assumed to be true and we find that the claimed conclusion would indeed probably be true under these conditions, then we say the induction is a strong one. Such a strong induction joined with premises that actually are true—again, somewhat like a valid deduction using true premises—makes for a cogent induction. Cogency, then, has its analogue in deductive soundness. Again, somewhat like deduction, a strong inductive argument that claims to use true premises with a probably false conclusion is an inductive argument that simply does not exist. The only production possible from this combination of components is a weak, and therefore uncogent, induction. The following diagram summarizes the parallels between deduction and induction.

Diagram
5.12

Deduction: validity + truth + soundness = certainty
Induction: strength + truth + cogency = probability

If invalidity or falsehood or unsoundness exists in deduction, then there can be no certainty. If weakness or falsehood or uncogency be demonstrated in induction, then there can be no probability.

Take care not to confuse deduction and induction in the senses we have considered them. Such confusion can work like this: an item is treated as though it were a matter of past deductive certainty, when it is not; then that item is claimed to have predictive probability for the future. Just think of all the matters of prejudice that fall neatly into that description. For example, it was once considered a matter of such past deductive "certainty" that women were not competent to vote or to own businesses. Logically, this was an attempt to isolate a deductive "certainty" in a past that never really existed and then use it as an inductive, predictive argument that still somehow was supposed to retain its character of infallibility. Of course, the whole argument was based on factual errancy and logical ineptitude. Likewise, illegitimate inductive probability was, for far too long, attached to the idea that applying leeches would cure sick people of various ailments. When this flimsiest of threadbare probabilities began to be treated in actual clinical practice as if it were a certainty, the days of bloodletting with leeches were immediately numbered.

Be aware that these examples of confusing deduction and induction make for clear illustrations of anti-pragmatic dogmatisms. The former example falsely claims, roughly, that "We have empirically observed that women are pathologically unfit to vote or to own businesses," and, clinging to a perverse certainty attached to this sort of empirical observation, dogmatically marches onward through all the evidence to the contrary, through all the counterexamples. The latter example, based not on empirical observation so much as on an antiquated theory of disease, was likewise tenaciously clung to in spite of what must have been an almost unbroken string of contradictory cases. To cling with a kind of inductive tenacity to a belief properly eliminated by deductive means, or to suppose tenaciously that a belief's survival through some degree of testing confers upon it eternal and ideal certainty, will impede pragmatic investigation. And this can defeat all our attempts at building up an effective ethics of the mind. Deduction and induction are powerful tools by themselves, and they are especially powerful when combined in our pragmatic logic of events.

6

Pragmatism and Choice

■ *To deepen our understanding of logical argument, this closing chapter will examine a mathematical controversy of the late eighteenth century involving pragmatism, as represented by Thomas Beddoes, versus mechanicalism as represented by James Harris. Bearing in mind the analogy of pragmatism to the evolutionary process of natural selection, we will reexamine the importance of abduction, its encouragement, and its control by pragmatic criticism, through which we develop an effective pragmatic ethics of the mind.*

I N THIS book we have considered as pragmatic matters not only examples of the subjects we study, whether formally in an academic setting or informally in our day-to-day lives, but also and most importantly the *methods* by which we come to know those subjects. All of this may have seemed but an elaboration of common sense; if so, it is hoped that what follows will continue for you in the same spirit.

The various illustrations and descriptions of pragmatism that we have used in previous chapters show that dogmatic or fixed or "surefire" methods of acquiring and developing human knowledge, though they may seem the easiest or most expedient means toward an immediate end, will not prove useful or successful in the long run if we desire genuine development of our knowledge, knowledge that survives because, as method, it is useful to us. Our study so far has described pragmatism as a thought process involving experimentation, trial and error, and predictive, inductive explaining or guessing. Our discussions about the nature of pragmatism urge a self-correcting process, deductive elimination of error, and an understanding of the method of pragmatism itself as a direct analogue of the workings of biological evolution by natural selection. Let us look again, and finally, at how all this may actually apply to academic subjects and to our daily lives. To do this, and to round out this work, three items discussed throughout this text in various, separate circumstances will now be succinctly brought back into play. They are posed as three questions.

- First, what is pragmatism, and how can it be understood as an analogue of biological evolution?
- Second, what is the nature of a hypothesis itself?
- Third, what are some of the components that play a role in the self-correcting exercise of pragmatism?

Of the various explanations of pragmatism given by Peirce himself, the following one, provided in a proposed 1907 article for *The Nation*, is entirely suitable for our present needs:

The method of pragmatism is simply the experimental method, which (taking the word "experiment" in its widest sense, so as to make it applicable to cases in which the fulfillment of the conditions has to be waited for instead of being artificially produced) is the invariable procedure of all successful science. Thomas Beddoes showed, as early as 1792, that it is the procedure even of mathematics. (Peirce 1907, MS 320:29)

Peirce here refers to Thomas Beddoes, M.D. (1760–1808), who championed an experimental approach to mathematics, as contrasted with the rote, mechanicalistic method espoused by universal grammarian James Harris (1709–1780). Recall from chapter 1 our use of the fourth proposition of the first book of Euclid's *Elements of Geometry*, which proposes that if two triangles are equal in certain components, then all the components and the triangles themselves are equal. Using this as an instructive example, Beddoes showed that by experimenting on diagrams suitable for the occasion students could actually see and genuinely understand how Euclid's demonstration proceeded, instead of merely repeating, parrot-like, all the steps of the proposition in the right order (see Stewart 1991 for a fuller account). Beddoes insisted that these active procedures were "mental experiments" requiring creative, pragmatic acts of genuine comprehension instead of the easily forgotten rote drillings favored by Harris, who smugly asked, "Who ever heard of *Logic*, or *Geometry*, or *Arithmetic* being proved [or learned] *experimentally?*" (See, respectively, Beddoes 1792: 18–19, and Harris 1771: 353.)

Which would you choose, in academic matters and in life in general: Beddoes' approach, "in which the fulfillment of the conditions has to be waited for," or that of Harris, in which the best one can hope for is knowledge that is "artificially produced"? Which method of acquiring and developing human knowledge, if the Harris option can really be called knowledge at all, will prove more secure and reliable? Is not the pragmatic option the obvious choice if we wish for future reliability and, especially, for *adaptability* in our applications of knowledge, whether within an academic or vocational setting or in further investigations of life in general? At least we can be confident that if the pragmatic option turns out to be a wrong one, it has available, as a *pragmatic* option, the power and the tools for self-correction, which can eliminate it from our further consideration. But that elimination itself, of course, would be simply another application of the pragmatic method, this time to itself.

Because we have cited biological evolution by natural selection as a testable hypothesis itself and have offered it as a living analogue of how we acquire and develop our knowledge, let us recall the workable understanding of it that we employed in chapter 1. Through the process of natural selection, some genetic stocks, by competition with their environment over time, will be more or less successful at survival. Although the subject of biological evolution is quite complex and has a long history, masterfully examined elsewhere (see Mayr 1982), the illustration we will consider here is deliberately ordinary and practical.

Let us suppose that the people of a neighborhood in an area of the world where mosquitoes carry malaria wish to rid themselves of the pests. "Compound XYZ" has been recommended to them, but, unfortunately, the people notice that even after repeated applications of Compound XYZ, many mosquitoes survive, in contrast to the label's stated claims of effectiveness. The community leaders contact the representatives of the chemical company producing Compound XYZ, who express immediate concern and send technicians to investigate. After confirming that the compound has been applied in accordance with the printed instructions and that, indeed, many mosquitoes are surviving, the technicians proceed with a plan to solve the problem.

Here is the experiment the technicians use to discover the answer. Bear in mind that the problem for the representatives of the chemical company is somewhat different from the problem facing the people who want to rid themselves of the mosquitoes. The company, if they wish to sell more of their insecticide, not only must provide these people with an immediate solution to their problem; they must also understand why and to what degree the mosquitoes are surviving. First, they capture and confine 2,000 mosquitoes. They expose 1,000 of them to the recommended concentration, a solution of 1 part Compound XYZ to 99 parts distilled water, and find that 100 mosquitoes survive, an unacceptably high number. The first part of their experiment concludes when, after hypothesizing that a stronger solution is needed, they discover that exposing the second group of 1,000 mosquitoes to a solution twice as strong produces excellent results, only ten survivors. The neighborhood is alerted to use the new recipe, the chemical company provides the amount of Compound XYZ at no additional cost, and the first part of the technicians' work is complete.

Yet they are not through with their investigation. They must now deal with a more fundamental question: Why is the new, stronger recipe necessary? To answer this question, they gather a group of 1,000 mosquitoes and repeat the exposure experiment.

Diagram 6.1

solution of 1:99 against 1,000 mosquitoes = 100 survivors

They now ask, "Why do 100, and just *these* 100 mosquitoes, survive?" And they further ask, "What will be the result if we allow these 100 survivors to reproduce and multiply to a population of 1,000, and then subject them to a stronger concentration of spray?" So, they generate a new group of 1,000 from the survivors of the earlier test and try the stronger solution, 2:98, of insecticide.

Diagram 6.2

solution of 2:98 against 1,000 mosquitoes = 100 survivors

And what of a still stronger spray on 1,000 descendants of this group of survivors?

Diagram 6.3

solution of 3:97 against 1,000 mosquitoes = 100 survivors

Assume that the technicians can continue these experiments up to a solution ratio of 99:1, ninety-nine parts of XYZ to one part of water.

Diagram 6.4

solution of 4:96 against 1,000 mosquitoes = 100 survivors
solution of 5:95 against 1,000 mosquitoes = 100 survivors
solution of 6:95 against 1,000 mosquitoes = 100 survivors
* *
solution of 50:50 against 1,000 mosquitoes = 100 survivors
* *
solution of 99:1 against 1,000 mosquitoes = 100 survivors

Here is the question the technicians must now confront: Are the 100 mosquitoes that are surviving the 99:1 solution identical with the beginning generation that could only survive the original 1:99 solution? Of course not. The phenomenon their experiment has produced is an example of biological evolution by natural selection, plain and simple, because each succeeding generation represents a "survival of the fittest" group of mosquitoes.

We may take this process as an analogy of how we test other conjectures, theories, explanatory hypotheses, wild guesses, erroneous notions, crazy ideas, and so forth, that describe our knowledge at any given point. This procedure is pursued through the use of hypothesis, which Peirce defines as follows:

A hypothesis is something which looks as if it might be true and were true, and which is capable of verification or refutation by comparison with facts. The best hypothesis, in the sense of the one most recommending itself to the inquirer, is the one which can be the most readily refuted if it is false. (*CP* 1.120)

As an example, Peirce offered the case of the seventeenth-century mathematician, physicist, and astronomer Johannes Kepler, who tried more than twenty differing hypotheses to describe the orbit of Mars before arriving at the one that seemed successfully to match the "facts" as revealed in the empirical observations of his predecessor, Tycho Brahe. Peirce described Kepler's overall effort as "the greatest piece of Retroductive [abductive] reasoning ever performed" (*CP* 1.74).

Peirce was certainly also aware that Kepler's whole procedure was a self-correcting, pragmatic one, in which a deductive elimination of errors inconsistent with the subject to be explained left the best surviving hypothesis, yet one that was capable of—and, indeed, demanded—further testing.

Kepler's work also offers a clear illustration of abduction, or the discovery, invention, and selection of hypotheses. Here is a fuller account of Peirce's remarks on the subject, found in his Harvard lectures of 1903:

Abduction is the process of forming an explanatory hypothesis. It is the only logical operation which introduces any new idea: for induction does nothing but determine a value, and deduction merely evolves the necessary consequences of a pure hypothesis. . . . Its [abduction's] only justification is that from its suggestion deduction can draw a prediction which can be tested by induction, and that, if we are ever to learn anything or to understand phenomena at all, it must be by abduction that this is to be brought about. No reason whatsoever can be given for it, as far as I can discover: and it needs no reason, since it merely offers suggestions. (*CP* 5.171; also Turrisi 1997: 230)

Kepler's work involved both of the senses of abduction that we examined in our chapter 1, namely, (1) the selection of a hypothesis from an already formed list of possibilities and (2) what we are now equipped to recognize as a *nonrational* flash of original insight. Kepler certainly had the already-formed hypotheses of Ptolemy and Copernicus to work with (see *CP* 1.72), but he found the idea that planets moved in perfect circular orbits, which both Ptolemy and Copernicus believed, inconsistent with Brahe's record of observations of the orbit of Mars. His moment of nonrational insight seems to have occurred when he saw that an ellipse bore a certain likeness to what appeared, from Brahe's recorded observations, to be the orbit of Mars. Since Kepler was such an outstanding mathematician, he probably had a considerable arsenal of mathematical hypotheses to choose from in demonstrating that the similarity he noticed really was a model of the actual orbit. Peirce gave an account of Kepler's work in his "Minute Logic" of 1902:

. . . at a certain stage of Kepler's eternal exemplar of scientific reasoning, he found that the observed longitudes of Mars, which he had long tried in vain to get fitted with an orbit, were (within the possible limits of error of the observations) such as they would be if Mars moved in an ellipse. The facts were thus, in so far, a *likeness* of those of motion in an elliptic orbit. Kepler did not conclude from this that the orbit really was an ellipse; but it did incline him to that idea so much as to decide him to undertake to ascertain whether virtual predictions about the latitudes and parallaxes based on this hypothesis would be verified or not. This probational adoption of the hypothesis was an Abduction. An Abduction is Originary in respect to being the only kind of argument which starts a new idea. (*CP* 2.96)

In attempting to verify his "virtual predictions," Kepler produced a sequence of twenty-two hypotheses leading to his final description of the orbit (see *CP* 5.362). So it seems that every truly successful abduction, in the sense of presenting a genuinely *testable* hypothesis, will in its moment of discovery and in the process of actual testing bring into view new groups of problems as well.

Merely *proposing* a testable hypothesis is very different from actually *executing* tests on it. An untested hypothesis cannot lead anywhere safely. And at least two irrational yet seemingly productive avenues can lead from an *un*tested or *un*criticized abduction, at least for a short distance. One of these avenues is the route of *relativism,* and the other is the route of *mechanicalism.*

In considering knowledge, relativism claims that there are no universal standards of or for rationality, objectivity, or—most importantly from a pragmatic point of view—method, and that such universal standards cannot exist (see Stewart 1994). We may likewise take this understanding to mean that one should have no hope whatever for such standards, even when, with errors and inevitable blank spots in the pursuit of knowledge, they are continuously sought and provisionally maintained. Thus, any holding to the belief that there may be universal or common-denominator principles in human knowledge is considered by at least one serious thinker, Paul Feyerabend, to be "conceited, ignorant, superficial, incomplete, and dishonest" (Feyerabend 1987: 25). From Feyerabend's point of view,

[I]t will become clear that there is only *one* principle that can be defended under *all* circumstances and in *all* stages of human development. It is the principle: *anything goes*. (Feyerabend 1975: 19)

For human knowledge, then, relativism says "anything goes." All supposed hypothetical solutions to problems are of equal value, whether within physics, or morals, or in the writing of philosophy books!

At the point of a nonrational abduction, that creative flash of insight into a problem or unusual phenomenon, like Fleming's insight that led to the discovery of penicillin, we might be prepared to say "anything goes." In fact, when we are first confronted with a problem that is absolutely new to us, we *should* provisionally adopt this attitude. But if we do not follow such moments with clear-headed pragmatic criticism, deductively eliminating contrary notions and applying not self-satisfied certainty but probability onto surviving explanatory notions, then we are left stranded among our "anything goes" abductions with *nothing but* "anything goes." Using this relativistic account of knowledge and its development, we might as well accept the belief of the Aetherius Society, founded in 1954 by Sir George King, that the Buddha and Jesus arrived here from Venus! If initial suppositions go uncriticized, this explanation carries just as much weight and credibility as any more conventional account. Abduction without subsequent testing thus does inevitably produce relativism: all possible explanations and hypotheses are of equal value.

In this book I have advocated pragmatism as the fundamental method underlying all other methods for acquiring human knowledge. This does claim a universal or common-denominator character for it. Does an intellectual procedure guided by pragmatism fit Feyerabend's damning description? Surely not, for how could a method like pragmatism, which is destined to self-correct even *itself* if it should fail as an explanatory hypothesis for human knowledge, be "conceited, ignorant, superficial, incomplete, and dishonest"? Assuredly, *we* may exhibit any or all of those traits as we employ pragmatism, or any other method for acquiring and developing human knowledge. But if we apply the method carefully and thoroughly to an investigative process as we use it, those lamentable traits can be controlled and perhaps eliminated from our procedures.

Mechanicalism, on the other hand, does not in the end embrace the multiple and at least occasionally contradictory claims of relativism, but instead settles in a usually haphazard way on a single hypothetical solution to a given problem and then dogmatically maintains it. The adherent to mechanicalism gathers alleged knowledge by means of what Peirce described in "The Fixation of Belief" as the method of tenacity (*CP* 5.384). We looked at this portion of Peirce's essay during our initial examination of realism, in chapter 1. Those who adopt the method of tenacity pick an attractive hypothesis or revert to one already present and, with all their might, hang onto it! They employ such an hypothesis unreflectively and mechanically; they pay no heed to conflicting evidence. Humoralism was maintained as a theory of disease in just this way. In fact, the ad hoc attempts to explain its failures were unwitting complaints about its mechanicalistic applications. Such "explanations" as, "We did not receive this patient early enough for sound bleeding to have been truly effective!" must have been among the excuses that humoral apologists offered.

As applied to human knowledge, mechanicalism teaches that the outcome of a given investigation can be completely, precisely, and *repeatably* determined in advance of actually undertaking the investigation. Mechanicalism implies that our knowledge, so called, is had in machine-like, exactingly formulaic, deterministic, predestinational ways. You can see how some aspects of this position are easily found in the relativist's procedures, and how a somewhat weak position of relativism likewise plays into the mechanicalist's hand. The relativist who says, in effect, "For any problem, all alleged hypothetical solutions are of equal value" must be enforcing this doctrine in a mechanicalistic way, otherwise the pragmatic criticism that thwarts relativism could arise. Likewise, the mechanicalist who selects what he feels certain is the one correct hypothetical solution to a problem surely selects such a pet theory in a haphazardly relativistic manner.

You will recall from an earlier point made in this chapter how James Harris was convinced that such a mechanicalistic approach was THE right approach for logical and mathematical operations, including the learning of them: "who ever heard of *Logic*, or *Geometry*, or *Arithmetic* being proved [or learned] *experimentally?*" (Harris 1771: 353) This trained-parrot approach to knowledge, which has not disappeared entirely since Harris's writing, takes pragmatic abduction out of account altogether. Its "abduction," the abduction of the mechanicalist about human knowledge overall, actually removes abduction in any pragmatic sense from the process of acquiring human knowledge. Thus, the mechanicalist's approach to knowledge not only forbids the posing of testable hypotheses but also ignores deductive and inductive criticism. In fact, the mechanicalist regards both criticism and abuction as unnecesary.

This is the very mechanicalistic tendency that we saw Peirce decrying, in chapter 3, in the extract from his 1900 article "Our Sense as Reasoning Machines." Recall his comment on one mechanicalistic approach in particular: "But so we do when we go irreflectively by a rule of thumb, as when we apply a rule of arithmetic the reason of which we have never been taught." Not only is that kind of rote application psychologically unsatisfying, it is also irrational. Peirce continued in that same context: "The irrationality here consists in our following a fixed method . . . so that if it does not happen to be right in its application to the case at hand, we go hopelessly astray" (Peirce 1900, MS 831: 9–11). The adherents of the humoral theory of disease, for example, exhibited such irrationality. And if following an uncriticized fixed method produces irrational consequences, the relativist's following of no method other than an uncriticized "anything goes" similarly produces irrational consequences. Transitions to the irrational seem unavoidable for both relativism and mechanicalism when their abductions, or seeming abductions, are maintained without pragmatic criticism.

Abduction, therefore, should retain its requisite but initially autonomous role within our pragmatic logic of events, our system of pragmatic criticism. As the phase of our pragmatic logic in which hypotheses are either rationally chosen or nonrationally discovered, abduction has an indispensable role to play. We cannot improve knowledge without abduction, but abduction alone, used uncritically, may well dispose us toward irrationality (see Stewart 1997).

Pragmatically speaking, we do not care logically where our hypotheses come from, assuming they are reasonably free of egoistic preoccupations and are not mere thoughtless repetitions of old recipes. In this sense abduction is the ability to *see the problem before us clearly, including its conceivable consequences.* If we cultivate the intelligence, background, curiosity, and initiative *to see* in this way, original explanations and hypotheses arise for us quite spontaneously, in an almost instinctual way (see Stewart 1997). Cultivating the ability to "see" like this is a fundamental element of knowledge, a fundamental part of cultivating a certain ethics of the mind, a *pragmatic* ethics of the mind. Deductive and inductive reasoning can be learned, but abductive reasoning, especially of the *non*rational sort we have looked at here, must be cultivated in all of its unpredictability as the initial and most creative stage of pragmatic inquiry.

Each discipline and field of knowledge, of course, has a subject matter and facts and hypotheses that are special to it. How clearly the pragmatic approach applies to each of these areas may seem to vary, but the common thread of pragmatism runs through pursuits as diverse as the fine arts and laboratory sciences, as seemingly disparate as the vocation of automobile mechanic and the profession of physician. That is, in all these areas we make guesses about the "facts and hypotheses" of that subject, retain for further testing those guesses that seem to fit the facts under examination, and freely discard those guesses that do not survive our testing. The ability to conduct efficiently the elimination of erroneous belief characterizes our much-desired pragmatic ethics of the mind, which we can apply to all areas of our lives.

Finally, let us remember the dangers associated with our unguarded emotions, even in the exercise of experimentalism and in the acquisition and development of our knowledge. All of us expect certainty or at least secure predictability in many of the things we think we know. We tend to form strong emotional attachments with some beliefs that we consider essential to us. When reinforced by our emotions, the result can be dogmatism.

The human tendency to cling emotionally to the irrational can be illustrated by a universal human experience in childhood. Virtually all children, unless truly unfortunate or terribly abused, develop a view of one or both parents that does not allow for either vulnerability or fallibility. No healthy child releases easily the security of belief in the larger-than-life image of a parent. We all cling tenaciously to those comforting notions that seem vital to our well-being, even in the face of contradicting evidence. Eventually, however, the healthy child bows before the accruing weight of evidence and begins the process of critical reevaluation, of cultivating a wiser, if less comforting, understanding of that parent and the role that good and vulnerable parents must play.

But the tendency to cling to long-held or comforting notions is not the province of children only. It is, unfortunately, a human tendency we never outgrow. Without the cultivation of pragmatic criticism, we remain at the mercy of that tendency to cling emotionally to ideas in which we have invested not only time and habits and hypotheses but to which we have attached assumptions about ourselves, others, and the world. A true and useful ethics of the mind will require us to confront that tendency, to take up and test new hypotheses without emotional predisposition and to be willing to rid ourselves of error, whatever the level of discomfort. That is exactly what the growing child eventually and involuntarily does and what adults must learn to do voluntarily, by force of will, by choice.

The notion that this ability to take up hypotheses, test them against that which we wish them to explain, and yet be willing to discard them in the event they do not work out involves a certain willingness to embrace error and fallibilism. This is yet another characterization of our pragmatic ethics of the mind. It also involves a willingness to submit the knowledge one claims to the scrutiny of experts, to become part of what Peirce called a "community of investigators." To be a member of such a community requires that you have at least some rudimentary understanding of the area under investigation and that you put your private desires, your self-serving ego, completely aside. The will to learn, then, is the beginning of the cultivation of scientific intelligence. In other words, one must have the moral and intellectual courage to test one's own beliefs, and to do so mercilessly. This latter requirement of a pragmatic ethics of the mind is crucial to the development of useful knowledge. But it is a requirement more difficult to cultivate than the mere will to learn. Without a sound ethics of the mind, even an ability to understand our questions and problems, much less to solve them, simply falters. Yet if successfully cultivated as a disciplined habit, such an ethical approach to knowledge can reduce or even nullify the dangers of excessive, dogmatic individualism and the sheepish acceptance of an ignorant consensus. This ideal condition of the "scientific man" is what Peirce extolled in the first of his Cambridge Conferences Lectures, "Philosophy and the Conduct of Life."

Nothing is vital for science; nothing can be. Its accepted propositions, therefore, are but opinions, at most; and the whole list is provisional. The scientific man is not in the least wedded to his conclusions. He risks nothing upon them. He stands ready to abandon one or all as soon as experience opposes them. Some of them, I grant, he is in the habit of calling *established truths;* but that merely means propositions to which no competent man today demurs. It seems probable that any given proposition of that sort will remain for a long time upon the list of propositions to be admitted. Still, it may be refuted tomorrow; and if so, the scientific man will be glad to have got rid of an error (Peirce 1898, MS 437: 16; *RLT*: 112).

If you approach the guesses and trials of human knowledge with sufficient intellectual courage and discover *for yourself* the pragmatic connections we have looked at, and if you learn to select and adjust pragmatically among the various subsidiary, adjunct, or contributing methods of acquiring and developing knowledge that we have examined, your ethics of the mind will be secure. You will then be, in whatever area or pursuit, "glad to have got rid of an error."

References

American Bible Society. 1854. *The Holy Bible*. 43d edition. New York: American Bible Society.

Aune, Bruce. 1970. *Rationalism, Empiricism, and Pragmatism: An Introduction*. New York: Random House.

Baldwin, J. M., ed. 1901–1905. *Dictionary of Philosophy and Psychology*. 3 vols. in 4. New York: Macmillan.

Barker, Stephen F. 1967. Geometry. In *The Encyclopedia of Philosophy*. Ed. Paul Edwards. New York: Macmillan, 1967.

Beddoes, Thomas. 1792. *Observations on the Nature of Demonstrative Evidence; with an Explanation of Certain Difficulties Occurring in the Elements of Geometry*. London: J. Johnson.

Brody, Boruch. 1967. Glossary of Logical Terms. In *The Encyclopedia of Philosophy*. Ed. Paul Edwards. New York: Macmillan.

Burke, James. 1978. *Connections*. Boston: Little, Brown.

———. 1985. *The Day the Universe Changed*. Boston: Little, Brown.

Clark, Ronald W. 1984. *The Survival of Charles Darwin: A Biography of a Man and an Idea*. New York: Avon Books.

Collingwood, Robin G. 1938. *The Principles of Art*. Oxford: Clarendon.

Copi, Irving M. 1982. *Introduction to Logic*. 6th edition. New York: Macmillan.

Descartes, René. [1911] 1973. *The Philosophical Works of Descartes*. 2 vols. Trans. Elizabeth S. Haldane, and G. R. T. Ross. New York: Dover.

Duin, Nancy, and Dr. Jenny Sutcliffe. 1992. *A History of Medicine*. New York: Barnes & Noble.

Edwards, Paul, ed. 1967. *The Encyclopedia of Philosophy*. New York: Macmillan.

Euclid. 1952. *The Thirteen Books of Euclid's Elements*. Trans. Sir Thomas L. Heath. Great Books of the Western World. Chicago: Encyclopædia Britannica.

———. 1956. *The Thirteen Books of Euclid's Elements*. 3 vols. Trans. Sir Thomas L. Heath. New York: Dover.

Feyerabend, Paul. 1975. *Against Method*. New York: Verso.

———. 1987. *Farewell to Reason*. New York: Verso.

Fisch, Max Harold. 1986. *Peirce, Semeiotic, and Pragmatism.* Ed. K. L. Ketner and C. J. W. Kloesel. Bloomington: Indiana University Press.

Gaunt, William. 1970. *The Impressionists.* New York: Weathervane.

Gillispie, Charles Coulston, ed. 1970. *Dictionary of Scientific Biography.* New York: Charles Scribner's Sons.

Harris, James. 1771. *Hermes.* 3d ed. London: I. Novrse & P. Vaillan.

Hurley, Patrick J. 1997. *A Concise Introduction to Logic.* 6th ed. Belmont, Calif.: Wadsworth.

Janson, H. W. 1966. *History of Art.* Englewood Cliffs, N.J.: Prentice-Hall.

Ketner, Kenneth Laine, with Arthur Franklin Stewart. 1984. The Early History of Computer Design: Charles Sanders Peirce and Marquand's Logical Machines. *The Princeton University Library Chronicle* 45: 188–224.

———. 1986. *A Comprehensive Bibliography of the Published Works of Charles Sanders Peirce.* Revised edition with expanded microfiche collection of Peirce's lifetime publications. Bowling Green, Ohio: Philosophy Documentation Center.

Macfarlane, Gwyn. 1984. *Alexander Fleming: The Man and the Myth.* Cambridge: Harvard University Press.

Marquand, Allan. 1886. A New Logical Machine. *Proceedings of the American Academy of Arts and Sciences* 21: 303–307.

———. n.d. Papers of Allan Marquand. Manuscript Division. Department of Rare Books and Special Collections. Princeton, N.J.: Princeton University Libraries.

Mayr, Ernst. 1982. *The Growth of Biological Thought.* Cambridge: Harvard University Press.

Mays, Wolfe. 1953. The First Circuit for an Electrical Logic Machine. *Science* 118: 281–282.

Meadows, Jack. 1989. *The Great Scientists.* New York: Oxford University Press.

Parsons, Charles. 1967. Foundations of Mathematics. In *The Encyclopedia of Philosophy.* Ed. Paul Edwards. New York: Macmillan, 1967.

Peirce, Charles Sanders. [1854–1914]. Manuscript collection. Texas Tech University: Institute for Studies in Pragmaticism.

———. ed. 1883. *Studies in Logic by Members of the Johns Hopkins University.* Boston: Little, Brown.

———. 1886. Letter to Allan Marquand, 30 December 1886. The Allan Marquand Papers. Princeton, N.J.: Princeton University Library.

———. 1887a. Logical Machines. *The American Journal of Psychology* 1: 165–170.

———. 1887b. Letter to Mr. J.M. Hantz of 29 March 1887, in the transcription by Max H. Fisch. Indianapolis: The Peirce Edition Project.

———. 1889. Definitions in *The Century Dictionary and Cyclopedia*. Ed. W. D. Whitney. New York: Century.

———. 1892. The Doctrine of Necessity Examined. *The Monist* 2: 321–337.

———. 1893. Reply to the Necessitarians. *The Monist* 3: 526–570.

———. 1898. Reasoning and the Logic of Things. MSS 437, 441, 439, 442, 443, 444–445, 446, 825, 951, and 948. Manuscript collection. Texas Tech University: Institute for Studies in Pragmaticism. (See Peirce 1992.)

———. 1900. Our Senses as Reasoning Machines. MS 831. Manuscript collection. Texas Tech University: Institute for Studies in Pragmaticism.

———. 1901–1905. Definitions in *Dictionary of Philosophy and Psychology*. Ed. J. M. Baldwin. New York: Macmillan.

———. 1907. Pragmatism. *MSS* 318, 319, 320, 321. Manuscript collection. Texas Tech University: Institute for Studies in Pragmaticism.

———. 1931–1960. *Collected Papers of Charles Sanders Peirce*. 8 vols. in 4. Ed. Charles Hartshorne, Paul Weiss, and Arthur Burks. Cambridge: Harvard University Press.

———. 1975–1979. *Charles Sanders Peirce: Contributions to* the Nation. 3 vols. plus Index vol. Ed. Kenneth Laine Ketner, and James Edward Cook. Lubbock: Texas Tech University Press.

———. 1976. *The New Elements of Mathematics by Charles S. Peirce*. 4 vols. in 5. Ed. Carolyn Eisele. The Hague: Mouton.

———. 1982–. *Writings of Charles S. Peirce: A Chronological Edition*. 30 vols. projected. Ed. Nathan Houser and (previously) Max H. Fisch, Edward C. Moore, and Christian J. W. Kloesel. Bloomington: Indiana University Press.

———. 1992. *Reasoning and the Logic of Things: The Cambridge Conferences Lectures of 1898 by Charles Sanders Peirce*. Ed. Kenneth Laine Ketner; Introduction by Kenneth Laine Ketner and Hilary Putnam. Cambridge: Harvard University Press.

Popper, Sir Karl Raimund. 1985. *Popper Selections*. Ed. David Miller. Princeton, N.J.: Princeton University Press.

Robin, Richard S. 1967. *Annotated Catalogue of the Papers of Charles S. Peirce*. Amherst: University of Massachusetts Press.

Robinson, E. 1955. Thomas Beddoes, M. D. and the Reform of Science Teaching in Oxford. *Annals of Science* 11: 137–141.

Sadie, Stanley, ed. 1980. *The New Grove Dictionary of Music and Musicians*. 20 vols. London: Macmillan.

Schnabel, Artur. 1969. Reprint. *Music and the Line of Most Resistance*. New York: Da Capo Press. Original edition, Princeton, N.J.: Princeton University Press, 1942.

Selby-Bigge, L. A., ed. 1902. *Hume's Enquiries*, 3d edition. Oxford: Clarendon.

Shannon, Claude E. 1938. A Symbolic Analysis of Relay and Switching Circuits. *Transactions of the American Institute of Electrical Engineers* 57: 713ff.

Stephen, Sir Leslie, and Sir Sidney Lee, eds. 1917. *The Dictionary of National Biography*. London: Oxford University Press.

Stewart, Arthur Franklin. 1991. Peirce, Beddoes, and Pragmaticistic Abstraction: An Introduction. *Southwest Philosophical Studies* 13: 75–88.

———. 1994. Objectivity in Peirce's Pragmaticism: Five Consequences for Relativism. *Southwest Philosophical Studies* 16: 84–96.

———. 1997. Peirce, Popper, and Putnam: Abduction, Reasoning, and Consequences. *Southwest Philosophical Studies* 19: 79–88.

Stock, John Edmonds. 1811. *Memoirs of the Life of Thomas Beddoes, M.D. , with an Analytical Account of His Writings*. London: J. Murray.

Turrisi, Patricia Ann. 1997. *Pragmatism as a Principle and Method of Right Thinking: The 1903 Harvard Lectures on Pragmatism by Charles Sanders Peirce*. Albany, N.Y.: State University Of New York Press.

Tuttle, Preston H. n.d. The Preston H. Tuttle Collection. Lubbock: Texas Tech University, Institute for Studies in Pragmaticism.

Williams, Cecil B. 1964. *Henry Wadsworth Longfellow*. New York: Twayne.

Whitney, W. D., ed. 1899. *The Century Dictionary and Cyclopedia*. 10 vols. New York: Century.

Index

a posteriori knowledge, 116
a priori knowledge, 108–9
abductive reasoning, xi, 22, 26, 28–32; in
    Euclidean geometry, 29; in the germ
    theory of disease, 29–30; Kepler's use
    of, 127–29; mechanicalism in, 129,
    131–32; and a pragmatic ethics of the
    mind, 133; relativism in, 129–30, 131.
    See also hypotheses
ad hominem attacks, 60–61, 62
algorithms, 89, 93, 97, 100
analogies, 49; inductive, 113–15, 118
arguments, 52–53; conclusions in, 53, 55,
    56, 73, 83–84; four-term arguments,
    90–93, 97–100; *modus ponens* argu-
    ments, 82, 104–5, 107; *modus tollens*
    arguments, 82, 105–7; premises in, 56,
    83; inductive strength of, 119–20. *See
    also* syllogisms
artistic expression, nonrationality in, 58,
    68–72
authority, arguments from, 60, 62

Baldwin, James Mark, 95, 97
Beddoes, Thomas, 123–24
beliefs, fixation of, 40–50; in artistic expres-
    sion, 58, 68–72; in emotional states, 58,
    65–67, 71–72; irrational, 56–57; nonra-
    tional, 58–72; rational, 55–56; in reli-
    gious experience, 58–65, 71–72

Brahe, Tycho, 127, 128

categorical syllogisms, 82, 83–89
cause and effect relations, 104–7, 116–17;
    necessary conditions, 106–7; sufficient
    conditions, 105, 106–7
certainty: in deductive reasoning, 27,
    84–85, 108–10, 120; practical vs. ideal,
    8–9
Church, Alonzo, 97
circular reasoning, 117
classes, logical relations of, 89–93
cogency, 119–20
common sense: applications and misappli-
    cations of, 34–37
community of investigators, 10, 12, 19,
    135
computer design, xi, 76, 93–100
conclusions, 56; deductive, 83–84; objec-
    tive, 53, 55, 73; subjective, 73
Copernicus, 128
creativity, 78–81
criticism, pragmatic, 12

Darwinism. *See* evolution
Descartes, René, 107–9
deductive reasoning, 26, 32, 82; Cartesian
    legacy in, 107–9; categorical syllogisms,
    82, 83–89; certainty in, 27, 84–85,
    108–10, 120; disjunctive syllogisms,

Arthur Franklin Stewart is director and editor of the
Center for Philosophical Studies at Lamar University
in Beaumont, Texas. He is an active author and editor who has published several articles and contributed to several previous books on C. S. Peirce.

ELEMENTS OF KNOWLEDGE

was composed electronically
using Adobe Garamond and Chianti BT types,
with displays in Castellar MT.
The book was printed on 60# Joy White Offset acid-free,
recycled paper and was Smyth sewn and cased into printed
Kivar 7 Chrome finish over 88-point binder's boards, with head and foot bands
and 80-pound matching endleaves, by Thomson-Shore, Inc.
Book and dust jacket designs are the work of Gary Gore.
Published by Vanderbilt University Press
Nashville, Tennessee 37235